Birdwatcher's Year

Ann Tate
Line illustrations by John Tate

BIRDWATCHER'S YEAR

DAVID & CHARLES
Newton Abbot   London   North Pomfret (Vt)

(title page) 'Trumpeter swans had produced young.'

For Barbara, John, Helena and Larry – with love and thanks

Black-and-white photographs by Ann Tate, Larry Tate, Dave Parfitt and The Wildfowl Trust
Colour photographs by Ann Tate and Martin B. Withers

British Library Cataloguing in Publication Data

Tate, Ann
  Birdwatcher's year.
  1. Birdwatching——Great Britain
  I. Title
  598′.07′23441   QL690.G7

  ISBN 0–7153–9191-7

Typeset by ABM Typographics Limited, Hull
and printed in Great Britain by
Butler & Tanner Limited, Frome and London
for David & Charles Publishers plc
Brunel House Newton Abbot Devon

Published in the United States of America
by David & Charles Inc
North Pomfret Vermont 05053 USA

Contents

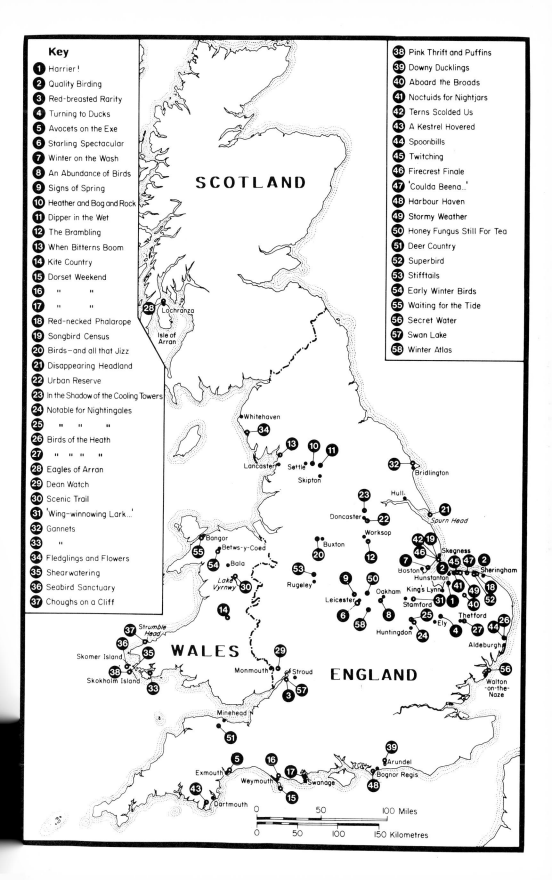

Key

1. Harrier!
2. Quality Birding
3. Red-breasted Rarity
4. Turning to Ducks
5. Avocets on the Exe
6. Starling Spectacular
7. Winter on the Wash
8. An Abundance of Birds
9. Signs of Spring
10. Heather and Bog and Rock
11. Dipper in the Wet
12. The Brambling
13. When Bitterns Boom
14. Kite Country
15. Dorset Weekend
16. "   "
17. "   "
18. Red-necked Phalarope
19. Songbird Census
20. Birds—and all that Jizz
21. Disappearing Headland
22. Urban Reserve
23. In the Shadow of the Cooling Towers
24. Notable for Nightingales
25. "   "   "
26. Birds of the Heath
27. "   "   "
28. Eagles of Arran
29. Dean Watch
30. Scenic Trail
31. 'Wing-winnowing Lark...'
32. Gannets
33. "
34. Fledglings and Flowers
35. Shearwatering
36. Seabird Sanctuary
37. Choughs on a Cliff

38. Pink Thrift and Puffins
39. Downy Ducklings
40. Aboard the Broads
41. Noctuids for Nightjars
42. Terns Scolded Us
43. A Kestrel Hovered
44. Spoonbills
45. Twitching
46. Firecrest Finale
47. 'Coulda Beena...'
48. Harbour Haven
49. Stormy Weather
50. Honey Fungus Still For Tea
51. Deer Country
52. Superbird
53. Stifftails
54. Early Winter Birds
55. Waiting for the Tide
56. Secret Water
57. Swan Lake
58. Winter Atlas

SCOTLAND

28 Lochranza
Isle of Arran

WALES

ENGLAND

Whitehaven
34
Lancaster
13
Settle
10
Skipton
11
32
Bridlington
23
Hull
Doncaster
22
Worksop
Spurn Head
21
Bangor
55
Betws-y-Coed
Buxton
20
42 19
Skegness
Bala
54
12
46
Sheringham
Lake Vyrnwy
30
53
Rugeley
7
Boston
2
45 47 2
Hunstanton
9
50
41
49 18
14
Leicester
Oakham
King's Lynn
52
6
8
31 1
Stamford
25
40
Huntingdon
Ely
44 26
24
27
Thetford
Aldeburgh
37 Strumble Head
36
29
56
35
Monmouth
Stroud
Walton-on-the-Naze
Skomer Island
38
33
3 57
Skokholm Island
Minehead
51
39
Arundel
5
16
Exmouth
17
Bognor Regis
Weymouth
Swanage
48
43
15
Dartmouth

0   50   100 Miles

0   50   100   150 Kilometres

Harrier!

East Anglia

'The weather's improving – to dreadful,' declared Dave.

For the past hour we had been standing at the top of a Norfolk heath in swirling snow. Now, at last, the snow was easing a little. It wafted, floating gently, settling softly. The wind had dropped and visibility was no longer close to 'nil'.

In winter we go, whenever we get the chance, to the east coast. We trudge the shingle banks, or slip and slither our way along muddy seawalls, or negotiate sand dunes, or sea-watch for 'fly-bys' from tall cliffs.

Buffeted by winds – or shrouded by mist – or hailed or rained upon, we binocular-scan the sea, the saltmarshes, the mudflats, the freshwater pools, the foreshore. A flock of snow buntings, a skein of brent geese, a flotilla of eiders, a great skua or a lone gannet makes it worth the waiting.

It has become a ritual to return via Roydon Common, for there is always the chance on this boggy stretch of heathland of wintering hen harriers. It is best to arrive an hour or two before the light grows dim. We are never the first. Others will have already staked a claim with tripods and telescopes.

There we all stand in companionable silence, stamping our feet, swinging our arms, pulling woolly caps down over ears, getting colder and colder as the skies darken. More folk tramp along the sandy track with their paraphernalia. Fingers and toes grow numb. 'In two minutes I'm going back to the car,' I keep muttering.

Then – suddenly – there it is. A ghostly pale grey shape rises from the woodland edge, fingered wings held typically in the shallow V: a male hen harrier. Low over the heath he flies, elegant, graceful. With a leisurely flapping of wings, or a soft gliding, the splendid bird rises above the skyline and disappears behind the trees. I let out my breath.

There he is again now, sailing low. White in the gathering greyness of dusk

Woolly hat and binoculars

'A favourite common.'

he quarters the shrubby ground. He turns, and now we see the contrast of black tips to the wings. In the grass below he sights movement. With a sudden drop-pounce, he plummets. Then, back up into the sky explodes the 'jump-jet' harrier and over the heath he sails.

The dark shape of a 'ring-tail' rises from cover. It joins the male and together they hunt. A *third* bird appears. We catch a shock of white above the banded tail. These white-rumped dark birds can be immatures – or adult females; difficult to tell apart and hence, colloquially, known as 'ring-tails'.

Now a blue-grey merlin, the smallest of the falcons, hurtles across the heath. It settles, to sit statue-still on a post. Half-an-hour later it takes off with swift darting flight and rapid wingbeats. A bonus.

The hen harrier is the commonest of our three harriers. But still sufficiently rare to be given special protection under the law. The breeding status of the marsh harrier and the Montagu's harrier in Britain remains precarious.

The hen harrier is also the least migratory of the three species, more able to tolerate the cold. Our wintering birds may have travelled south from British breeding grounds, or arrived, cross-Channel, from the Continent.

But wherever they have come from, I have no doubt that, as winter approaches once more, we shall again be standing, frozen to the marrow, on that blasted heath – waiting for the weather to improve to 'dreadful'.

Quality Birding

North Norfolk Coast

We stood on the high shingle bank, striving to keep our balance. A force eight wind was blowing straight into our faces, making it difficult to hold binoculars steady. Waves crashed deafeningly on to pebbles beneath. The temperature was below zero. Snow was forecast. I was very glad of my thermal vest, three layers of woollies, and waterproof and windproof outer garments. We were seawatching, hoping for red-breasted merganser, Slavonian grebe, black-throated diver, auks, sea ducks . . .

'Prepare for a squall,' warned our leader. 'See those kittiwakes?'

Far out, a sprinkling of small white birds swooped up and down in hurried flight before an ominous sky-darkening. Two minutes later hailstones painfully whipped our cheeks and we retreated hastily into the comparative shelter of the landward (saltmarsh) side of the shingle bank.

'You can always tell kittiwakes by their great swoops. They sense a squall and flee before it.'

It is said that the north Norfolk coast is the best place in England to see birds of passage – and to meet well-known birdwatchers. Bryan Bland is a 'well-known birdwatcher'; we (the Royal Society for the Protection of Birds Leicester Group) had borrowed him for the two days of a winter weekend.

'Is it quantity – or quality – you are after?' was his first question that morning.

'Quality,' decided the majority. Rarities are fun. So grapevine contacts were consulted, location of latest new arrivals checked on, hunches followed, and an efficient itinerary worked out to make the very best of the limited time available.

'Glaucous gull at Salthouse.' We drove the short distance along the A149. There, on the edge of mud flats, was a mixed flock of gulls. But which one was the glaucous?

'Large size, square flat head, huge wicked-looking bill, pearly grey mantle, pure white bunched primaries, no black: that's the glaucous. Iceland gulls also have white wing tips, but they are smaller, with gently domed heads and less massive bills. Here, I'll show you.'

Bryan took up his drawing board and, with a few quick strokes of his black felt-tipped pen, he drew outlines of the bills, head shapes and size differences of the two gulls to make all quite clear.

We were soon to discover that he specialises, not only in deft, on-the-spot sketches, but also in brief pungent descriptions with much use of cunning metaphor. Identification of birds is never easy; novice birdwatchers need all the help they can get.

'Why won't the bird stand sideways, nicely in profile, looking to the left – just as it does in my field guide?' we ask. 'How can we tell whether the wretched creature's legs are red or not, if it won't come out from behind that clump of grass?'

Birds are so inconsiderate. They perch too far away in bad light. Males and females are often differently befeathered. Plumages change according to season. And rarely do individuals deign to oblige by giving us that nice, clear view of white rump, dark eyestripe, or green speculum we are so anxious for.

Bryan's aim was to wean us off complete reliance on precise diagnostic features, and to get us to concentrate on the 'personality' of each species; on the way it holds itself, feeds, moves, calls; its general behaviour and first-glance appearance – 'jizz' for short. ('Good word that for a Scrabble board. Worth a lot of points,' muttered someone.)

Field guides are handicapped by the pocket-size requirement. Now was our chance to learn some of those useful tips which have to be omitted from their pages and which a really experienced birdwatcher acquires for him/herself over years of serious looking and listening.

'Lapland bunting' was top of our shopping list. Off we drove to Wells-next-the-sea. But how were we to tell apart these winter visitors from Greenland and the ridiculously similar (according to the handbook's artist) reed bunting?

'Lapland buntings look like *squashed* reed buntings,' said Bryan. And they did; all flattened and crouched, creeping low in the grass; quite unlike the sprightly reed with its flashy habit of fanning out the long tail to show off white outer tail feathers.

At Holkham we looked hopefully up into the pine trees planted long ago to help stabilise the sand dunes, and we 'pished'. 'Pshwishwishwishwish,' we whistled (with backs of hands pressed to lips) hoping to entice possible firecrest, siskin, brambling. A great spotted woodpecker flew curiously over, tits of several kinds moved in close and a very tame robin appeared, to accept crumbs from an outstretched hand.

In the car park we eyed the puddles in the tarmac where parrot crossbills sometimes drink after a meal of sticky pine seeds. The big-headed silhouette with its strangely twisted mandibles surprises motorists on a day out to the seaside. But the lone pied wagtail today would raise no eyebrows.

We drove back towards Titchwell Marsh, stopping to look out over the miles of saltmarsh on the way. There, in the far distance, were wintering geese. Several species. But how to tell?

'The brent [German *brand* = burned] goose looks as if it has stuck its head and neck up a chimney and emerged sooty black – although with a little of its "clerical collar" still clean. See the white mark on its neck? The smoke analogy holds well for flying brents too. Look for a factory chimney cloud – or a wisp of smoke curling across the sky; that will be brent geese. They are small enough not to have to fly in V-formation to get "lift" like the larger geese.

'Now sort out the pink-footed goose from the bean goose by shape. Both

Siskin

have a very dark head and neck. But the pink-footed looks as if someone has pushed a tennis ball up into the top of a short sock: round head, short neck, with a small beak stuck on. Whereas bean geese have long stocking necks with longer heads, longer bills.

'White-fronted geese? They're the ones that could have been made up from a kit, I always think, each part clearly demarcated (bill, box-like head, neck) – a rather angular goose. Greylags, by contrast, have thick necks and large heads merging into a huge triangular bill in one more or less continuous line.'

We squelched through the oozy wet mud of the long sea wall at Titchwell Marsh. We looked down to see goldfinches and snow buntings feasting on fallen seeds in the heaped litter of saltmarsh plants: sea lavender and sea purslane.

The goldfinches pecked neatly and precisely. The snow buntings burrowed energetically, discarding dead stalks and leaves with a quick flick of the head; then dug deeper to get at the hidden seeds, their busy movements leaving visible impressions. The bright red and yellow colours of the goldfinches contrasted with the subtle brown, grey, chestnut and white plumage of the snow buntings.

A short-eared owl beat low over the saltmarsh on long rounded wings. It braked, twisted, pounced – and resumed its to-and-fro search, the owl species most likely to be seen, in Britain, hunting by day.

We reached the beach. Mussels had colonised the remains of an ancient forest and we asked about waders, so busily taking advantage and feasting there. With a few well-chosen words and a quick sketch or two, Bryan sorted them out for us. Redshank or spotted redshank? we asked. Bar-tailed godwit or black-tailed godwit? Golden plover or grey plover? Dunlin or little stint?

White-fronted geese

Waders in winter plumage are *not* easy.

Back at Cley, a long-tailed duck rested on Arnold's Marsh. But where was the 'long tail'? It was a female, explained Bryan, and only the male proudly carries the two extra long black tail feathers.

More ducks. 'Eiders are the ones with Roman noses falling off the tops of their heads. Tufted duck and scaup are similar in plumage but the latter's heavier, more angled head and larger bill give it a less cuddly look; a tufted duck would make the more suitable "soft toy" for a toddler. Goldeneye have heads which look like blobs of dough scooped up from the bench and *plonked* on.' (And they did).

The useful epithets continued: black-headed gulls are 'spiky'; common gulls have a 'benign' look; the wingtips of herring gulls are 'polka-dotted'.

We walked along the shingle bank – and it was then the blizzard hit us. But it had been a good day. We retreated, as dusk fell, to the warmth of 'The George and Dragon'. We talked on – but not for long. There was the possibility of kingfisher and water rail for early risers on the morrow. A trip to Hunstanton Cliffs was planned for fulmars, and to Holkham for Egyptian geese.

Collectively we saw just over one hundred species (102) in the two days. So, in the event, both quality *and* quantity were achieved.

Red-Breasted Rarity

Slimbridge New Grounds, Gloucestershire

On our arrival at the Wildfowl Trust Refuge, we headed straight for the STOP-SPOT board in the foyer. 'January 22nd,' we read. '9.00am. Red-breasted goose in front of Loke Hide.' It was now 10.30am. . . .

We hurried past the Big Pen. And one of the first birds we saw? 'Surely that's a . . . ?'

'. . . red-breasted. But one of Sir Peter Scott's tame ones.'

Only thirty-odd *wild* red-breasted geese have ever been recorded in Britain. They breed in Siberia and, in September, fly south. But this one, like the others, had strayed too far to the west, away from its regular migratory route. At first light on Tuesday, 17 January, a wide-awake Warden scanned the flock of white-fronted geese grazing on the banks of the Severn estuary – and found the exciting stranger in his telescope. And it was still here.

We walked the length of South Finger with its series of wooden hides. Conceived and built as one unit they give good views of the Top and Bottom New Pieces, the Tin Shed Grounds and the Four Score Field. We were screened from the wild birds as we hurried along behind high earth banks planted with willow. On the far side lay a large scrape, created by the removal of earth for the banks and much appreciated by incoming wintering ducks and waders.

We reached Loke Hide. *'Birds have ears'*, read the stern notice at the entrance. We tiptoed past, not daring to whisper even. Talking in a loud voice whilst approaching a hide is the guaranteed way to become an expert in identifying the back ends of birds flying off in a panic.

Inside the hide it was crowded: in fact there was a queue. A considerate Warden was letting each person in turn peep through his telescope.

Miles of saltmarsh stretched before us, reaching to the shores of the River Severn. But closer to, in a large field enclosed by hedges, 2,750 white-fronted geese grazed. Somewhere in amongst them was a lone red-breasted, perhaps the world's most beautiful goose?

'See the gate,' directed the Warden in a low voice, 'count the posts to the right, one, two, three. There: third post, eleven o'clock. See it? Bother, it's put its head down, I've lost it. No, wait a minute . . .'

It was my turn for the telescope. 'Come forward from the second post,' I was directed, 'to the left of that group of six . . . it's lifted its head. Now!'

And I saw it. A bold white flank stripe was the give-away. The chestnut red neck, and the distinctive black and white patterning of the back and head and belly were clearly visible as neighbouring geese spread themselves to either side.

'Approach the hide quietly.'

The world population of red-breasted geese has decreased this century. Hunting and habitat loss are the most likely reasons. Changing agricultural policies have transformed former wintering grounds, bordering the Caspian Sea, into cotton fields – which are shunned by the geese. A resulting westward shift in winter quarters could mean that British sightings will occur with greater frequency in the future.

Curiously, the decline of the peregrine falcon may also have affected red-breasted goose numbers. The geese seek protection from their enemy, the arctic fox. They build their nests close to an eyrie; because they have learned that peregrines are highly efficient at driving away foxes? Janet Kear writes – in *Wildfowl World*, No 84 – 'We assume that the peregrine is "programmed" not to hunt near its nest (if it did it might feed on its own young) and that this immunity extends to the goose and its goslings.'

Because the red-breasted goose is clearly a bird in urgent need of special conservation measures, Slimbridge Wildfowl Trust has long hoped to breed from its collection. Success was very limited until, in the summer of 1983, a colleague discovered the secret. Triumphantly he promised four breeding pairs from his own small collection to the Trust. But first the staff at Slimbridge set about creating a faithful replica of his garden: water spaces, land areas, nesting boxes, feeding devices – all were as near as possible the same. The geese moved in, felt at home, laid eggs – and a most satisfactory twenty-four goslings hatched that year.

But today, from Loke Hide, we were looking at a single *wild* red-breasted goose. It had arrived in the company of a flock of Russian white-fronted geese.

A white-fronted goose can be identified by the small white blaze on its face at the base of the bill. Plumage is grey-brown in colour, neck feathers are furrowed and there is distinctive dark barring on the belly. White-fronted geese also breed in low-lying, shrubby tundra. Each winter flocks return to Slimbridge, the largest congregation of the species in Britain.

The presence of a very occasional *lesser* white-fronted goose from Scandinavia on the reclaimed land of the Severn is well-known to have been a crucial factor in Sir Peter Scott's choice of site for the new wildfowl refuge and research station he had dreamed of creating during the War. The 'lesser' is smaller, with a pinker, shorter bill and a yellow ring around the eye. A 'birder's bird', it is one of the most difficult species on the British List to identify at a distance.

Slimbridge today attracts both 'twitchers' and 'birders'. It draws people who come for a fun day out and it provides for the serious ornithologist. Beginner birdwatchers brush up on their identification of British ducks, geese and swans in the European pen with borrowed binoculars; the more advanced tackle the two hundred foreign species; research students arrive from Universities to write theses.

Grandparents introduce grandchildren to the simple pleasures of 'feeding the ducks'; photographers and artists appreciate views of birds in close up; the visually handicapped can follow a braille trail; the disabled have their own boardwalk and comfortable hide; the Tropical House offers an impression, in miniature, of a tropical rainforest where brilliant humming birds hover at hibiscus flowers.

Red-breasted goose

But, right from the start, Sir Peter's wish has always been to attract truly wild birds close enough for people – lots of people – to enjoy. And today, in one of the large hides, we were getting splendid views of *geese*.

The white-fronted geese, when they arrive for the winter, spend nearly all the hours of daylight grazing on the banks of the River Severn. I could see them now, slowly advancing and snipping off, scissor-like, the vegetation.

The STOP-SPOT red-breasted rarity had been swamped again and was now hidden from view. The next person to look through the telescope would be less fortunate than myself.

'See the post where the little owl has perched?' said the helpful Warden, 'call it twelve o'clock, try coming down to a quarter past, near those three lapwings . . . there's a chance . . .'

Lesser white-fronted goose

F·E·B·R·U·A·R·Y

Turning to Ducks

The Ouse Washes, Cambridgeshire

'You'll have good views today,' the Warden of Welney Wildfowl Trust Refuge told us. 'The light is just right.'

The Ouse Washes are about twenty miles long and half-a-mile wide. In summer they are grazed by cattle. In winter they act as a safety valve when the two straight bordering rivers, dug in the seventeenth century by a Dutchman, Cornelius Vermuyden, become swollen with rain and overflow. Torrents of water pour into the Ouse River System, sluice gates open and excess water floods the meadows. High dyke banks keep the surrounding agricultural land free from flooding. In fly wetland birds from the far north – to winter on the Washes.

The Warden pointed out the most likely spot for short-eared owls on the hunt for stranded voles, told us that there were plenty of fieldfare about, and said it was a good year for ruff.

We walked the long, covered-in wooden bridge which led us over the Hundred Foot River to the members' observatory. Through the large plate-glass windows (a pleasant feature of all Wildfowl Trust Centres) we looked out on to a deep lagoon, dug especially to attract wild birds.

Graceful white swans – the resident mute swan, and the wintering Bewick's and whoopers with their black and yellow bills – sailed to and fro, or upended to feed, or preened ruffled feathers on islands. The whooper and the Bewick's had survived a 2,300-mile flight from Siberia, families arriving together. Pairs greeted noisily, neck-stretching, head-bowing, wing-flapping.

And there were the ducks. 'From troubles of the world, I turn to ducks . . .' wrote F. W. Harvey, the poet.

Handsome drake mallards swam with their dowdy mates in tow. 'By December each year,' said our expert, 'most male mallards are already in breeding plumage. Pairing and courtship follows.'

The mallard is the first of the ducks to swop dowdy eclipse plumage for

Ouse Washes

breeding plumage: bottle-green head, curly tail, white neck ring, rusty breast
and blue speculum. Of all the European ducks, the mallard's breeding season
lasts the longest – which accounts for its undoubted success as a species. We
were near enough to compare the drake's greenish-yellow bill, with his mate's
orange (it is the female mallard which alarm-quacks the loudest).

Tri-coloured pochards with chestnut heads, glossy black chests and pale
grey bodies paddled beside grey-brown mottled females – and then upped and
dived smoothly, disappearing under water to bob up again many yards
distant. And black and white tufted ducks tacked to-and-fro, the wind
blowing their crests into stiff little top-knots.

We left the observatory and followed on behind the willow-planted
screening banks into which small fibre-glass hides were set. 'Don't let your
heads bob up,' had warned the Warden, 'or the ducks will take fright'. And
we didn't. From the hides, shimmering water meadows, fingered spits,
islands, orange-tinged osiers and countless bobbing birds lay exposed to view.

There were waders, too. Snipe – striped plumage camouflaged the colour of
dead winter reeds – probed the mud with bills bizarrely long. A flock of dunlin
flew across the marsh in a silver swirl, catching the sun, dazzling the eye.
Handsome green plovers pattered at the edge with round floppy 'lap' wings
and jaunty wisps of headcrests. Seven ruff, without as yet their elaborate
courtship adornments, fed at the northern tip of a dyke.

The Ouse Washes is the largest inland area of regularly flooded marshland in Great Britain. So important is it to wintering wildfowl, that it is included on the International List of Wetlands of the RAMSAR Convention and must be especially safeguarded against threats of reclamation for farmland and industry, and against over-shooting by wildfowlers. Fortunately, more than half the area is now owned by conservation bodies.

The hours passed swiftly. I recall the amazing blue of a fieldfare's sunlit back (drab grey on a grey day); the tantalising glimpses of a secretive water rail which crept and scuttled in the shelter of a ditch (red bill, black and white striped flanks, richly streaked brown back, bluish-grey neck); and the rusty red flanks of a redwing which shot up in front of me as I walked past willow scrub behind the barrier bank.

A pair of black-tailed godwits flew low over the reedbeds. Two cormorants landed on posts and stood black and gaunt. A little grebe paddled with surprising speed through the water. Black-headed gulls with red legs and red bills loafed on small islands.

And more ducks. The Warden was right about the light. The pale winter sunshine enhanced duck colours perfectly. The aquamarines, sienna browns, yellow ochres, greens, purples and turquoises of plumage were sensational against the 'silver meadow' background of glittering water.

Hundreds of wintering wigeon grazed at the water's edge, tinted-pink breasts, yellow Mohican-hair-piece crowns glowing gold. The whistling of the males carried far across the water-logged land, a wild and haunting sound: 'Peee-yoo, peee-yoo.'

And there, the smallest duck, a teal. It bobbed, bright yellow triangle on its tail, metallic green eye patch and white 'Plimsoll line' above the wing.

Wigeon

Near by, boldly patterned shovelers filter-fed, swooshing their odd-looking spatular bills through the shallows.

A lone pair of gadwall preened on shrinking tussocks. The drake, speckled and freckled, showed a rectangular blaze of white wing band. Slim, elegant pintails rose suddenly from the water and flew, a small flight of nine, the curving white line on slender necks and the long tail feathers clearly visible.

We watched until the light began to dim – and then we returned to the observatory. The Warden at dusk each day distributes grain, a supplementary food supply. In flew the ducks, crash-landing, splash! – up-ending, tail-wagging, bill-dipping, wing-flapping, dabbling, diving, quacking, gobbling, waddling along the edge. ('Ducks are comical things. . .')

Next time it rains hard back in the Midlands, I shall remember that February fill-dyke day. I shall imagine the water pouring in torrents into the Ouse River System, sluice gates opening and excess water flooding over the meadows to create the shimmering acres once again. And I shall picture all those thousands of appreciative ducks – and swans and waders – in their safe winter quarters; and forget for a while 'the troubles of the world.'

Avocets on the Exe

River Exe, Devon

The mouth of the River Exe is the largest and most important estuary for birds in the south-west peninsula of Devon and Cornwall. It is of international significance for its numbers of wintering wigeon, ringed plover and black-tailed godwit. In winter too, that elegant bird, the avocet, is to be found on the mudflats of the Exe; each year since 1947 it has returned in increasing numbers.

The best way to see the avocets, enticed back to breed in Britain forty years ago by the Royal Society for the Protection of Birds, is by boat. And how better than to join the RSPB's own 'Avocet Cruise'? Each winter, from December through to the beginning of March, cruises are organised on the Exe for close views of waders and wildfowl. And this year, I found myself in Exmouth, with members of my local RSPB group, boarding the *Devon Princess II* at 1pm on the last Saturday in February.

Our guide was Stan Davies, the Regional Officer for the South-west. 'I'd like to welcome Leicester, Huddersfield and Welwyn Garden City.' Stan's voice came over the loudspeaker as we left the quay and headed seawards. He told us that the end of February is the peak period for avocet numbers, 'record count so far this year is 170 birds.'

Then he went on to warn us that, during the cold snap earlier in the year, ice floes had swept in from the sea dragging buoys from their moorings. 'The

Captain is having to rely on his memory to negotiate the channel.' Help! Low tide is the best time to see birds from a boat – and low tide, especially the very low tide of early spring, is the best time to get stuck on a sandbank!

But there were no ice floes around today. It was as warm as summer, the temperature an amazing 15.5°C. So warm that we had earlier seen a comma butterfly on the wing. We'd been warned to bring thick clothing but now found ourselves stuffing woolly hats into pockets and loosening scarves.

'Shag on the rocks ahead; red-breasted merganser diving for fish near pink buoy; sanderling running along the edge of Dawlish Warren.'

We chugged past the famous Dawlish Warren, a sandy spit, rich in wildlife, which juts out across the mouth of the Exe. At the edge of dunes is a two-storey hide, open to the public, which gives wonderful views of the estuary and its birds – for those not lucky enough to be aboard a boat.

'Maer Rocks, to your left. Dark-bellied brent geese feeding on seaweed.'

Maer Rocks is where children love to paddle in the pools in summer. In winter it is given over to turnstones, purple sandpiper, oystercatchers and other shellfish-eating birds. But at this time of the year brent geese are also to be found foraging. Their favourite eel grass supply is used up and they must turn to other sources of food – including the farmers' cereal crops on fields inland. But very soon now the brents would be flying back to their breeding grounds in Arctic Russia. Except for some of the younger birds, Stan told us, which stay on until April. The dark-bellied brent goose is small, neat and sooty black, with white neck streaks and a white stern. Almost half the world population of brents winters in estuaries around the British Isles, nearly 100,000 birds.

The boat veered and, leaving the sea behind, headed upriver. Stan pointed out Cockle Sands, mega-feeding area for many waders. Through our binoculars we focussed on grey plover, curlew, redshank, dunlin, bar-tailed godwit. *Black*-tailed godwit we would see later, at the mouth of the River Clyst.

As we had been warned, our progress was punctuated by the boat grinding to a halt where the water shallowed. Were we to be trapped there until high tide lifted us off? No, each hitch was only temporary – and the few minutes of unplanned stillness was welcomed by photographers. Oystercatchers on a mussel bank; a small party of goldeneye; a pair of eider duck; three wing-stretching cormorants. Pintail, shelduck, teal. Cameras clicked away. Then off we would go again, chugging upriver.

Stan's commentary continued. 'Slavonian grebe' had everyone rushing to starboard. Slavonians, with their black caps and white cheek patches, are the most maritime of our grebes.

'Possible great northern diver': more excitement. But, as we drew closer, it turned out to be a great crested grebe. 'Well, you can't win 'em all,' said Stan.

He told us that during the January 'freeze-up' there had been a great influx of shelduck. Numbers were less now. Wigeon, too, were dispersing northward.

'The boat headed upriver.'

Four miles up, past the fallow deer in the grounds of Powderham Castle, past Lympstone with its red sandstone cliffs, past the eyesore high-rise blocks where Prince Edward rejected his career with the Marines – until we were below Topsham.

The sun was low in the sky now, shimmering the mudflats in a golden glow – and there were the graceful avocets, sweeping long curved bills from side to side through the fine silt, scooping up their favourite opossum shrimps and ragworms: a marvellous sight. But then, as RSPB members we were bound to be biased! We hoped some of these beautifully marked black and white birds were from our own RSPB Minsmere Reserve in Suffolk; others could be from Holland . . .

The tide was rising. The boat turned. The wind blew off the sea and it was growing cooler. Herons stood incongruously on tops of trees in the large heronry – as if super-glued. Already they'd built their nests; even would have laid eggs, said Stan. Two, standing below in the shallows, showed off bills tinged with orange – a sign that they were breeding.

Greenshanks were flying over to their night-time roost in the park. Hundreds of gulls circled above Dawlish Warren; numbers would build up to thousands by dusk. Skeins of dark-bellied brent geese flew down-river after a daytime of feeding in fields. And red-breasted merganser headed purposefully out to sea – as our four-hour boat trip came to an end.

Over 2,000 people enjoy an Avocet Cruise each winter. Hot pasties and hot drinks are served below deck at the bar, a comfort on chilly days. In Stan Davies, who has written his own booklet on the wildlife of the River Exe, we had an excellent guide. And we came away with a true understanding of the value of the estuarine habitat. The RSPB is ever on the alert, ever vigilant, for estuaries are constantly under threat – which means that the thousands of wintering birds they support are threatened, too.

Starling Spectacular

Abbey Park, Leicester

It was almost dusk on a February afternoon and we stood with Will Peach, 'Starling Man', in Abbey Park, a 73-acre green space in the centre of Leicester. For the last hour between half-a-million and a million starlings – impossible to estimate accurately – had been flying in from every direction. From daytime feeding grounds up to twenty miles away, they converge on Abbey Park to roost for the night.

The gigantic roost first hit the headlines in 1979: '50,000 starlings . . . foul droppings piled high on paths . . . whitewashed bushes . . . branches broken . . . tremendous noise . . . disgusting stench . . . picnic tables ruined . . . Abbey Park a wasteland.'

The years passed and each winter the starlings returned, numbers building up to a peak in March. All manner of scare devices were tried – bright lights, tapes of starling distress calls, a tame fox, water hoses, flares, fire crackers, dogs – but to no avail.

The City Council, faced with the noxious problem, decided to grant-aid a study of starling biology in the hope that a long-term solution might be found. Leicester Polytechnic's Will Peach, a biology graduate, was chosen to head the Council-sponsored 'Starling Squad'. And tonight Will was with us to tell us a little of his work.

We walked along paths slippery and evil-smelling. Corrosive droppings produce a 'grey acid' effect on the soil's ecology, killing plants and shrubs.

'Forty per cent of holly bushes have been lost,' said Will, 'and trees are actually being uprooted by the weight of the birds as they land on the branches.'

In the first year of the study the Starling Squad, under licence from the Nature Conservancy Council, wing-tagged over 1,500 birds. Noise and lights were used to drive the starlings into an 18-foot long net suspended on two 30-foot poles and held aloft. 'Sometimes,' Will told me, 'so many starlings flew into the net at one time, that the men holding the poles were knocked over backwards!'

Each bird was carefully removed to be aged, sexed, weighed, measured (more northerly populations have longer wings) de-loused and released. A florescent orange tag was fixed to the left wing of females and to the right wing of males. Juveniles were given yellow tags. The tags, stuck on with tape, were expected to stay in position for up to three months.

Sexes can be told apart by bill and eye colour. The male starling has a steel-blue tinge to the base of its bill and the female, a pink tinge. (Blue for a boy, pink for a girl!) The eyes of the male are a uniform dark brown; a pale-ringed iris distinguishes the eyes of the female.

That winter Leicestershire folk were astonished to see starlings with – it appeared – *orange* wings feeding on their bird tables. Seven hundred reports of sightings were phoned in to the Starling Squad, to be pinpointed on a map of Leicestershire. The birds were feeding at all compass points around the county, as had been suspected.

The Squad also put numbered rings on 2,500 birds. Some of the individuals they trapped were found to be wearing rings already. Recoveries since prove that Abbey Park starlings come from Russia, Finland, Holland, Belgium, Norway and Sweden – and areas of Britain.

So 1984/5 had been a winter of hectic activity for Will and his group. And to their – admitted – bafflement, the following year the starlings stayed away! Had all that netting and noise been sufficient deterrent? Large roosts were reported elsewhere in the county, but Abbey Park remained a pleasant place. Children played on unpolluted grass; old age pensioners sat on dropping-free seats; shrubs and trees began to recover. The Council congratulated itself – and congratulated the Starling Squad. But too soon.

The roost was slow to build up in autumn 1986 but, by now, February 1987, numbers were as high as ever.

As we stood beneath white-washed trees, Will spoke admiringly of his study-bird. 'Highly organised, great exploiters, supremely adaptable and efficient . . .' Probably the world's most successful bird.

The starlings' daily routine in the Park begins at dawn. The birds awake and 'converse'. The twittering gradually reaches a crescendo – then, quite suddenly, the exodus begins. Flocks leave the roost in waves. Wave after wave of starlings take off at short 2–3 minute intervals, with a great roar of whirring wings. Blackening the sky, they move out from Abbey Park in well-defined flightlines to feeding grounds. In late afternoon the return flight begins.

The sun was low on the horizon now and the birds were still flying in from 'pre-roost assembly points'. More than twenty of these points have been documented around the county. The starlings gather, the noise increases in volume then – suddenly – *whoosh!* Flocks rise, swirl and head for the city. The silence that follows their going is as extraordinary as the overhead formations themselves.

We watched as flocks swirled over the Park's outer perimeter, performing astounding aerial manoevrings. What is the secret of their superb synchronisation? Like spiralling clouds of smoke thousands of birds swept and soared, stunt-riding the sky. At invisible signals they dropped into trees, then rose again to stream upwards, circle, and resettle. The noise was immense. What is the purpose of it all?

A sparrowhawk appeared – and all hell broke loose! And another. Birds of prey must be attracted from miles away by the spectacular aerobatics. It is a mystery why starlings, expending precious energy by doing so, choose to overfly suitable roost sites *closer* to daytime feeding grounds. Do they gather in such huge numbers to learn from each other the whereabouts of the best food sources? Do they 'communicate' in some way?

Now it was dusk. Towards the central area of trees and bushes starlings streamed, alighting on branches which swayed under the weight. They settled, great clumps of blackness outlined against the sky. Starling literature suggests that each bird prefers its own 'personal space' at the roost, but photographs taken by the Squad show examples of individuals squatting close, touching, huddled for warmth.

This year Will and his team, under the supervision of Dr Jim Fowler, are fixing radio transmitters to the feathers of a number of individual birds to monitor behaviour by radio-tracking. They hope to find clues to the structure of the highly complicated social organisation which hints at a hierarchy with 'leaders' and 'subordinates'.

I left Will Peach to yet another night of work in the Park. 'You sound *fond* of those starlings,' I said. Perhaps there are Leicester citizens who will feel just a little sorry if the bird we all love to hate were ever banished; no longer to amaze us with squabbling antics in the garden, purposeful flightlines at the end of day, noisy pre-roost assemblies – and starling spectaculars at dusk.

'Starlings flew in to roost.'

M·A·R·C·H

Winter on the Wash

Freiston, Lincolnshire

Winter can be a cruel time for waders on the Wash. We found tragic proof of this on the most bitter 1 March for many years. Freezing mud. Temperatures down to −10°C. Ice on the sea. Scrunchy snow underfoot. Piercing east wind.

We were walking along the sea wall at Frieston in Lincolnshire, possibly the coldest place in England that day (we learned later). Frieston is on the north coast of the Wash. We had driven through Boston with its 'stump', the incongruously tall church tower visible for miles, and then parked in a car park not far from the wall. We struggled to the top and faced the sea.

Saltmarshes with winding creeks, and a great expanse of mudflats lay exposed: wide, uncluttered, beautiful in their loneliness. Behind us lay bleak fenland with its fertile silty soil which, since the Roman times, has been reclaimed by degrees for agriculture.

Well-lagged though we were, the wind made our eyes water and the cold eventually penetrated – however many the layers of clothing. But visibility was good and the birds exciting.

Dunlin twisted and turned in fast-weaving silvery flocks. Skeins of brent geese flew over. Parties of knot pattered on the icy mudflats. Ringed plovers scurried in their busy way. Eider ducks bobbed offshore, dodging the ice floes. Handsome shelduck swooshed in the shallows.

Lapland buntings and skylarks swirled and settled, searching for the last seeds of saltmarsh plants below the bank. Sea aster, sea purslane, sea lavender and glasswort fruit late in the year and provide winter sustenance for small seed-eating birds. A pied wagtail flew across and landed, its long tail shivering. What insects would it be finding on such a bitter day?

Not all memorable sightings were on the seaward side of the wall. A merlin was hunting inland, a small agile bird of prey, skimming low over the fens on narrow pointed wings. All telescopes and binoculars swivelled at the first shout of 'Merlin!' and trained on the dashing raptor.

Sheep sheltering below the wall huddled together for warmth. Behind them were miles and miles of inhospitable flat land criss-crossed with reed-fringed frozen dykes and patched with snow, blown into drifts by the ceaseless wind.

Our first tragic find was a kittiwake. The smallest of the British gulls, it lay dead in the snow, pale grey and white plumage, grey cheek patch, greenish bill, short black legs; quite frozen and in near-perfect condition – as if stored in an open air deep-freeze. Usually kittiwakes are seen only far out at sea in winter; this one must have been blown inland, to die.

After that we found more dead birds, their beauty still unspoiled. Grey plover: ash grey with feathers white-tipped, the diagnostic dark patch of feathers beneath its wings. Redshank: uniform speckled brown-grey with some white on tail and wings, orange-red bill and orange-red legs.

The next find gave us the chance to see at close quarters an auk, a fine winter-plumaged guillemot. Poor thing, it too was quite frozen. Auk 'wrecks' can occur in a hard winter. Many birds die and individuals are washed up on to the shore.

Another dead redshank. Another grey plover. The walk was becoming depressing.

'We found a dead guillemot.'

The Wash in winter is of outstanding international importance for many waders and wildfowl. Peak numbers occur between December and the beginning of March, when continental birds in their thousands are forced to move westwards across the North Sea in a desperate attempt to escape harsh weather conditions.

Four rivers flow into the great bay, the Ouse, Nene, Welland and Witham. The large expanse of mudflats and sandflats are rich in the invertebrate life upon which so many of the hungry birds depend: ragworms, tellins, laver spire shells, cockles and crabs.

Redshank are particularly vulnerable in cold weather. If the mudflats freeze over, it is impossible for them to find sufficient food. Wildfowlers would like to get redshanks back on to the list of birds which can be legally shot. But so far the Government has resisted, deciding that this species is already under too much pressure. Curlews, too, are still protected in spite of the shooters' wishes. The disturbance and fear men with guns cause spoils the tranquillity of wild lonely places for both birds and birdwatchers. And, as we were seeing heart-breakingly today, nature itself is enough of a challenge to birds.

The colder the temperature, the more fat reserves a bird needs to maintain body warmth. As its energy is used up in trying to keep warm, so its need for food is greater. But the frozen ground cuts off many birds, particularly waders, from their normal food supplies. They fall back on reserves of muscle protein to balance the high rate of heat loss – and still cannot find sufficient food. Thousands die.

We looked to see if BTO rings were present on the legs of the grey plovers, the redshanks, the guillemot and the kittiwake. No; no rings. Licensed ringers trap, ring and release birds in many countries. Had our redshanks come to winter on the Wash from breeding grounds in the Pennines? or from Iceland? Could our grey plovers really have flown all the way from Arctic Siberia? Where had our gull and our auk spent the summer?

By now we were feeling pretty frozen ourselves, in spite of the fact that a pale sun had appeared, shimmering the mudflats and glinting the snow. It was time to replenish our own fat reserves. Hot soup? That was what we needed. At Freiston Shore there is a hostelry well known to birdwatchers where they do a good pub lunch . . .

An Abundance of Birds

Rutland Water, Leicestershire

Through one of the glass panes in Plover Hide I could see a twite: a plump little linnet-like bird, brown, streaky-breasted, with a bright yellow stubby bill. And for once, I could feel I really deserved him.

We were on Egleton Reserve, the lagoon area of the Rutland Water Nature Reserve, and we had spent a blustery March morning wielding billhooks to create 3-foot long sticks from coppiced pussy willow branches.

The Warden had said, as he took a stick and pushed it firmly into its prepared hole, 'Cut a piece off a tree and you've got another tree for free.'

I found this astonishing bit of information difficult to swallow – but he was the expert; 40,000 fine upstanding saplings were sprouting on his nature reserve and many of these, he declared, had grown from stout twigs cut by past billhook-swinging volunteers.

Now and again I stopped to stretch my aching back. It served as excuse for a quick survey of the choppy water below. Mallard, teal, tufted duck, pochard, great crested grebe. Possible goldeneye? Possible gadwall? Possible pintail? I would have to wait until later for a proper look.

As we worked, we heard fieldfare 'chacking' from a hawthorn hedgerow. Devouring the last of the berries were redwing, too. Hedge-hopping yellowhammers proved another diversion and a flock of blue tits flickered and contact-called, 'psi-psi-psi', from the willows down by the water's edge. It was all very distracting.

Until the opening of the Kielder Reservoir, Rutland Water was the largest man-made stretch of water in the whole of Britain. So large, that when plans to flood their lowland were first announced, the Rutlanders protested, 'But we do not wish our county to be just a towpath around a lake!'

This made all concerned feel very guilty. It was decided by the authorities that the building of the dam across the valley was a 'regrettable necessity' – but they determined to make as satisfactory a job of it as they could.

So, as villagers sadly began to dig up bluebell and primrose roots from the soon-to-be-flooded little woods of their pleasant countryside and to plant them elsewhere on safer ground, the Anglian Water Board asked Dame Sylvia Crowe, the landscape architect, to take on the challenge of turning the proposed 3,000-acre inland sea, with its 27-mile perimeter, into an 'environmental asset'.

Contoured hills hide car parks tucked away in the hollows out of sight – for the cars of yachtsmen, fishermen, ramblers and birdwatchers. Raised knolls give picnickers panoramic views. And the planting of native trees and

Goldeneye

understorey shrubs, such as guelder rose, hazel, dogwood, spindle and blackthorn, has created new woodland, providing lush cover for birds.

When water levels drop the shoreline remains green, for it is seeded with a special grass which can survive being submerged for weeks at a time. Flood-tolerant species of willow and alder on the reservoir margins carry the tree-cover down into the water. Little winding paths run through woodland and across sheep-grazed sward. And the dam is turfed on the landward side to give it the appearance of a gently sloping field.

From the start, naturalists agreed that the western end of the reservoir, with its nine miles of shoreline along two arms, would make an excellent nature reserve. Positioned well away from the planned recreational activities, it promised to attract an abundance of wildlife – and so it has turned out.

The Leicestershire and Rutland Trust for Nature Conservation were given overall responsibility for creating the reserve – and did not shirk the task. A management agreement was signed with the Anglian Water Authority, some financial assistance and early help was given at the start of the project. But now it was up to volunteers to tackle the necessary labouring jobs.

So here we were, a group of local members of the Royal Society for the Protection of Birds, and we had been 'labouring voluntarily' all morning. Naturally, with no reserve of our own in the county, we are much interested in what goes on at Rutland Water. Sufficient money was quickly raised to buy the materials necessary for the construction of Harrier Hide; a sponsored birdwatch in competition with the Leicestershire and Rutland Ornithological Society and the Trust resulted in enough money for a new wader scrape; and work parties regularly turn up to take on any job that Tim Appleton, the Warden, asks of them.

'Last time we came, back in February,' reminisced a companion, 'snow lay on the ground. Tim had us clearing out overgrown scrub. We built a huge bonfire and soon unfroze.'

Today, the result of our labours was several long rows of planted saplings which, in ten years' time, will have grown into a grove of pussy willows doing useful service as a screen for walkers. The grove will attract, especially if regularly coppiced (as planned) robins, wrens, tits, dunnocks, blackcaps, redstarts, warblers . . . perhaps even nightingales?

At midday we made our way to Plover Hide for our promised reward: an afternoon's birdwatching. Specifically designed to make birdwatching easier for the disabled, Plover Hide is close to the car park. A ramp leads up to a wide sliding door. Inside is comfortable seating and adequate space has been left for the positioning of wheelchairs. Paned windows, instead of the more usual draughty gaps, make for warmer viewing.

Plover Hide is one of thirteen hides, all situated at sites regarded as particularly rewarding from a birdwatcher's point-of-view. ('Tim won't be

Great spotted woodpecker

satisfied until he's got wall-to-wall hides,' one weary hide-constructing volunteer was heard to mutter.) But it was worth all the hard work. Fifteen thousand birdwatchers visit annually and enjoy hides with a variety of views; there is a choice of woodland, herb-rich meadow, rank grassland, sheltered lagoons, reedbed and open water.

There was plenty to see from our vantage point. Although the first drops of water only officially began to trickle into the basin in 1975, Rutland Water is already famous for its wildfowl numbers. And already it holds the record in Britain for the inland stretch of water with the highest number of bird species in winter.

Thousands of wildfowl wing their way across northern seas to the Wash, follow the windings of the Rivers Welland and Nene – and discover this wonderful expanse of welcoming water. And there, at one end, is an undisturbed refuge planned especially for them. The wader passage in spring and autumn is also outstanding; on several occasions nineteen species of wader have been recorded on the same day.

'Building the three lagoons was an engineer's nightmare,' Tim told us as we munched our sandwiches. 'The instinct of engineers is to bulldoze and construct in straight parallels. I wanted *wiggly* lines.'

He asked for – and got – zig-zagged inlets, undulating banks, jagged spits, curving creeks, irregularly shaped bays and shallow scrapes. Scattered islands, with a variety of 'toppings', were constructed from surplus soil and waste.

Today flotillas of contented shovelers, tufted duck, gadwall and goldeneye bobbed about outside the hide in their secluded sanctuary. Gadwall numbers are particularly exciting. Each autumn Rutland Water holds the biggest concentration of gadwalls in Britain, over 30 per cent of the total population.

Cormorants wing-stretched on shingle banks. Waders – redshank, snipe, dunlin – probed in the wet mud. Gulls gathered at reed humps. Teal and mallard dabbled behind wave-preventing barriers. Wigeon grazed on the far shore.

Each year brings more exciting 'firsts' for the reserve; first wintering birds, first breeding pairs, first birds of passage.

On the occasions of my own visits I always manage to see something new when I visit Rutland Water: a preening water rail in full view below Lax Hill, four buoyant, saw-billed goosanders showing off their diving skills, short-eared owls roosting at dusk on the fence posts of the Hambleton Peninsula, a pair of displaying great crested grebes presenting mutual gifts of waterweed . . .

And today, most satisfying of all, for I felt that I and my billhook had really earned him – the stubby-billed twite.

Kingfisher

Signs of Spring

Charnwood Forest, Leicestershire

We went to the hills to look for signs of spring. It had been snowing and, although the snow melted quickly in the lowlands, up here on the heights there were still extensive patches.

So it was ideal tracking weather and prints abounded. Tiny tell-tale marks showed where voles and mice had scampered through grass tunnels roofed with snow to reach the safety of their homes. Small forepaw prints and long slipper-like hind prints: a rabbit had bunny-hopped in search of food. And we could smell the strong pungent scent of a trotting fox as we trailed dog-like paw marks.

No sign of squirrels at ground level, not a print, not a glimpse of a bushy tail. But when we looked up into the trees, we could see their dreys; untidy rounded twiggy 'nests' tucked into forks between branch and trunk.

We followed a path through the bare trees. Each tree had its fine strip of snow where the sun had not yet reached; thin lines running vertically, white against the darkness of green-lichened bark; lightning-conductor-like clues as effective as a compass: north-east was the direction they faced.

Yellow gorse blossomed further on in the open, a cheerful show of colour. Alders were handsome with last year's dark woody cones and this year's green catkins – still tight-closed with no sign yet of pollen. And there were more catkins: fluffy golden tails on the hazel trees and furry silver tufts on pussy willow.

The first bright green leaves were unfolding in a hawthorn hedge beneath which a pair of blackbirds flirted and 'chooked'. A song thrush sang its repetitive phrases from the top of an oak tree. Lower down, on the same tree, coal tits flickered in the branches, seemingly as happy upsidedown as right way up, constantly on the move, making it a challenge to spot that diagnostic blotch of white feathers on the nape.

We found a mossy stump with droppings on it. Again we played detective. Droppings are good clues. Rabbit, we decided. A sweet chestnut lay close by, its glossiness marred by decisive incisor scratch marks. What had interrupted the meal? Fox, again, most probably, said Doreen, our tracks-and-signs expert. Those of us with sensitive noses caught the rank whiff.

Now we were in woodland territory. In a fenced-off tree nursery had been planted young saplings: rowan, hazel, sallow, oak, ash – all local, traditional broadleaves. The ground was thick with the green of bluebell shoots. Pushing their way up through the soil with force they pierced the fallen leaves. We

Mallard and chick

Hazel catkins   *Witches' broom*

stepped carefully. In two months' time the slopes would be a vista of hazy blue.

Bluebells are indicators of ancient woodland. Since World War II, over half of Britain's ancient woodland has been destroyed. Fortunately, this particular bluebell patch is in the safe keeping of the Leicestershire and Rutland Trust for Nature Conservation.

We looked for further clues. Someone found a hazel nut split neatly in half. Were the markings on it caused by beak-blow? or tooth-nibble? The characteristic gnawed groove and the hole in the top where long incisors had been inserted proved that there *were* squirrels about – said Doreen.

The repeated call notes of a mystery bird puzzled. We scanned the trees and caught sight of the black cap of a great tit. We had heard it 'belling' earlier; this was another of its reputed forty utterances. The yellowhammer's song, a few minutes later, was a little-bit-of-bread-and-no-chees-ily recognisable. Robins and blackbirds also sang spasmodically, welcoming the pale March sunshine. A sulphur yellow butterfly, the early-year brimstone, flew along the line of the hedge.

Circling a frozen pond, we made our way uphill to rocky outcrops. Through the bracken ran a well-used path and in the snow were distinctive paw marks.

Badger! Our most exciting find yet. We followed the tracks, the folk in front trying hard not to obliterate the prints (bear-like pads, five neat little toe marks, impressions of sharp claws) for those behind.

They led to a sett. It was huge. We could see at least twelve entrances to what must be a labyrinth of tunnels. Some holes had dug out mounds of earth beside them, and heaped up piles of discarded hay and bracken. In all probability there were young cubs below, born back in February, and their sleeping quarters must be kept warm and dry. Soiled bedding is removed and fresh material is collected, by both boar and sow. Held close to the chest, the bundles are dragged backwards down into the chamber for the babes (up to five in a litter) to snuggle up into. Suckled for eight weeks, cubs would soon now be emerging, to romp and play above ground.

We looked for more badger clues. Scrapings in the soil showed where earthworms and grubs had been searched out. Well-marked tracks led in a number of directions, one straight towards a low gap in a stone wall.

The song of a chaffinch rang out loud and clear; a dunnock joined in; wheezy notes of greenfinch; exuberant shrilling of a diminutive wren; and a tree pipit took off from a boulder and 'tseep-tseeped' down in slow descent.

Birdsong, remnants of snow, prints of small mammals, new-opening leaves, catkins, the first green shoots of bluebells, and badger cubs: all most welcome signs of *spring*.

Chaffinch

A · P · R · I · L

Heather and Bog and Rock . . .

Malham Tarn, Yorkshire

'Once upon a time there was a little chimney-sweep, and his name was Tom . . .'

The opening line of *The Water Babies* is familiar to us all. We remember how, very early in the morning, Tom came to sweep the chimneys of Harthover Place, a great house 'built at ninety different times, and in nineteen different styles'. Mr Grimes led the way round to the back door and 'the ash boy let them in, yawning horribly'; soon Tom was 'in pitchy darkness, as much at home in a chimney as a mole is underground'.

The Harthover Place of the story is believed to be Malham Tarn House in the limestone country of Craven. Charles Kingsley wrote of 'the great grouse moors . . . heather and bog and rock, stretching away and up . . .'. Across these moors today stride walkers of the Pennine Way, a route which passes close by Malham Tarn.

'Harthover Place' is now a Field Studies Council Centre and one April I enrolled for a 'spring birds' weekend.

On arrival I surveyed (as everyone must do) the chimneys. Not the same ones, surely, as those swept by poor Tom? Behind the house rose Highfold Scar; in front, the lawn slopes to the tarn.

We were early risers on the first morning. In woodland we stood and listened to the vociferous dawn chorus. It's the early birdwatcher that catches the best bird song. Were these the woods, I wondered, that Kingsley had in mind when he wrote of Tom's escape from Ellie's little white bedroom? ('Tom, of course, made for the woods. He had never been in a wood in his life; but he was sharp enough to know that he might hide in a bush, or swarm up a tree . . .'.)

The wood in Kingsley's time contained many foreign and coniferous species, introduced by an earlier, eighteenth-century owner. Today there are plans to recreate and manage a 'wilderness woodland' of native trees and shrubs. As elderly trees succumb, young saplings are being planted to take

40

their place: hazel, mountain ash, wych elm, oak, beech and the beautiful 'bird-cherry with its tassels of snow'. (Kingsley, again.)

Through the trees shimmered the 150-acre tarn. We heard the growling call-note of great crested grebes. In a sheltered bay three pairs patrolled the water; and very handsome they looked with their new spring feathers: black crests and chestnut tippets.

Tufted ducks bobbed, still in the small compact flocks of winter. Black dome-shaped backs of coots. A pair of goldeneye and a pair of goosander.

We walked back up the track. Tiny pink female flowers sprinkled the branches of a larch; soon soft green needle-leaves would appear. A smart cock chaffinch was fiercely chasing a rival out of his patch. Two blackbirds sang against each other across a territory boundary. A courting robin offered his 'intended' a worm and she accepted with an excited quivering of wings. And a cock pheasant flapped its wings vigorously, shook its bright red wattles, and squawked, 'Kor*ok*, kor*ok*'.

We ate a hearty breakfast and then set off for the moor. ('. . . there were rocks and stones lying about everywhere . . . as he went upwards, it grew more and more broken and hilly . . .'.)

We could see on limestone crags the sooty marks left by Tom in his desperate bid to escape. Black lichen? All right!

Wheatears signalled their presence with a white flash of tail: spruce little summer migrants. 'Pee-*wit*, pee-*wit*': tumbling, twisting lapwings. One was already sitting on its nest, the white marks on the face and the white underbody visible as the bird crouched in the open on rabbit-nibbled grass.

Behind a grey stone wall lay a little pool. Redshanks bathed splashily and a very smart dunlin stood on guard. ('Clear and cool, clear and cool, by laughing shallow and dreaming pool'.) Beside small pools on upland moors is where dunlin come to breed.

On the road back to the tarn we passed a cluster of cottages. Below meandered a little stream; the stream believed to be the source of Charles Kingsley's inspiration.

One day – so the story goes – whilst staying on a walking and fishing holiday with friends, he was asked by the village schoolmistress to mind a group of local children. He took them for a stroll along the banks of the stream.

I wonder how good he was with children? An ordained clergyman, he became a chaplain to Queen Victoria in 1859. By 1863, the date of the publication of *The Water Babies*, he had been appointed Professor of Modern History at Cambridge. He was interested in politics and wrote tracts. Over-long stretches of moralising and politicising mar his fairy tale, written 'to inspire love and reverence for nature', and it sells more commonly today in an abridged version.

But perhaps he pointed out to those village children the caddis fly 'on four fawn-coloured wings, with long legs and horns'; and the dragonfly with 'eyes so large that they filled all its head, and shone like ten thousand diamonds'.

'A cock pheasant squawked.'

Maybe they saw 'little water-trees, starwort and milfoil and crowfoot'; and 'green caterpillars which let themselves down from the boughs by silk ropes for no reason at all'; and 'great spiders with crowns and crosses marked on their backs'.

The little stream flows into Malham Tarn. 'Tom lay down on the grass and looked into the clear, clear limestone water, with every pebble at the bottom bright and clean, while the little silver trout dashed about in fright at the sight of his black face; and he dipped his hand in and found it so cool, cool, cool; and he said, "I will be a fish; I will swim in the water; I must be clean, I must be clean".'

We walked alongside the stream and then negotiated the board-walk which led us safely across a treacherous bog to the shores of the tarn. Golden kingcups were in flower. A red grouse skimmed low over the heather. We heard, like Tom, 'the skylark saying his matins high up in the air'. A flock of eight curlew rose and we were treated to a spectacular display flight of steep flapping rises, slow glides and bubbling trills.

We couldn't leave Malham country without seeing the Cove and we made a detour in the mini-bus. 'Instead of soft turf and springy heather, he met great patches of flat limestone rock, just like ill-made pavements . . .' wrote Kingsley. Tom negotiated these 'ill-made pavements' and stood at the top of Malham Cove. With church bells ringing in his tired head he looked down and saw, 300 feet below, the woman in the red petticoat.

Down the curved cliff of the dried-up waterfall he climbed: 'But, of course, he dirtied everything terribly as he went. There has been a great black smudge all down the crag ever since . . .'. We looked – and there was!

'But,' warned Kingsley (and these are his concluding words) 'remember always that this is all a fairy tale, and only fun and, therefore, you are not to believe a word of it, even if it is true.'

Dipper in the Wet
Wharfedale, North Yorkshire

'The birdwatcher should lose no chance of improving his ear,' wrote E. M. Nicholson in 1931. Even when the line on the barograph shows no sign of an upturn and forecasts a wet, cold, blustery day?

Clad in waterproofs and wellies, we walked alongside the fast-flowing River Wharfe. Its steep slopes were wooded and, in spite of the rain, birds were singing. April: time of amorous chasings, ritual courtship, suitors' squabbles and bird song at its most vibrant. April is the best month to become familiar with the outpourings of resident birds, before the influx of summer migrants swells and complicates the chorus.

We stood on a bridge, looked down – and saw our first dipper of the day. On a moss-covered rock *dipped* a portly little black and brown bird with an eye-catching expanse of white on its breast. (To find a dipper, look for a bobbing white shirtfront.) It slipped into the water, disappeared beneath the surface and, fifteen seconds later, bobbed up again and hopped back on to the rock.

A second little amphibious songster whirred across stream, calling, 'Zurp, zurp, zurp.' It landed on an alder tree root; in its slightly upturned chisel-beak was held a long-legged cranefly. It dipped and dipped and flew under the bridge to feed its brood. Dippers begin to sing and to stake out their linear territories as early as November; to display and pair in January; and to lay the first of two – or three – clutches of eggs before the end of March.

In spite of the rain trickling down our necks, our spirits lifted. We had started the day in style. The dipper is a typical bird of upland rivers and one species we had very much hoped to see. We were to see three more pairs that day.

We crossed over the bridge and followed the wet and muddy path along the bank. Trees, still leafless, offered little cover as yet; another advantage of birdwatching in April. The lack of foliage made it easier to focus, with binoculars, on individual songsters: chaffinch, blackbird, song thrush, mistle thrush, wren, dunnock, blue tit, great tit, coal tit, nuthatch and treecreeper.

'A dipper with a white shirtfront.'

'This is *my* bit of Wharfedale,' each male sang, 'and I intend to entice a wife and raise a family – so all you other blokes, *keep out*.'

The mix of calls was confusing, but Edward Jackson talked us through. A blackbird sang from a hazel tree with swinging yellow catkins; buds were just beginning to open into miniature bright green leaves. 'The blackbird's song is varied, longer phrased, melodic, flute-like, often ending with a flourish.'

He pointed out a mistle thrush on the topmost branch of a very high tree. 'Short, clipped phrases; a brief pause between each rounded, mellow sequence; limited in variety in comparison with the blackbird; far-carrying quality.'

And a song thrush on a beech with long slender brown buds still tight-closed: 'Repetitive: repeated simple phrases, repeated single notes, bold and obtrusive.'

I fished out the 'soft cloth for binocular wiping' from my pocket yet again. The lenses of my binocs were rain-smeared and blurry, but the cloth – actually a clean handkerchief – was already wringing wet. So I delved beneath my anorak and pulled out a corner of shirt. Dry, thank goodness. A hasty wipe and a sort of visibility was restored.

Just in time. A flirting tail on the far shore promised excitement: grey back, pale yellow on breast, deeper yellow under tail, black line of folded wings. It was a grey wagtail. We could see by its black bib that it was a male; the female's throat is unmarked. 'Zissick, zissick,' it called and darted across the shingle after winged insects at the water's edge. Another uplands river bird.

Wharfedale is a traditional site for nuthatches. We soon saw – and heard them. If nuthatches are present, they let you know. We distinguished three calls: the territorial trill, 'Dididididi'; a clear, ringing contact call, 'Pui, pui, pui': and another, faster, 'Pi-pi-pi-pi-pi'. 'The chestnut on the flanks is usually darker in the male,' said knowledgeable Edward.

Spring flowers dotted the banks: pink blooms of butterbur, dainty white wood anemones, yellow coltsfoot. Above us, tiny rounded tits sang high-pitched, squeaky phrases, two-note chants, as they acrobated up and over twigs, peering at the underneath of fat green sycamore buds for grubs.

We walked on, reaching the Strid, a narrow channel of deep foaming water which spectacularly churns and leaps its way between gritstone ledges worn into weird shapes. Close by, a willow warbler flicked jauntily from one overhanging twig to the next. Not a resident bird this time, but our first – and only – summer migrant of the day. 'First of the year for me,' said Edward. The date was the 13th. We stood listening for its soft, rippling warble, and were soon rewarded.

By now most of us had tucked our binoculars away inside anoraks out of the wet. We had become bird *listeners*. We listened for contact calls, threat calls, alarm calls, begging calls, display calls, soliciting calls.

The trees were thinning now. Wild moor and gritstone crags lay ahead. An oystercatcher piped. We crossed another bridge and walked back along the opposite side: bitter-sweet robin notes; wheeze of greenfinch; 'chook, chook' of blackbird; 'huit' call of chaffinch; trill of wren.

A pair of pied wagtails alighted on the path. Two little black and white faces, two long bouncy tails, but the male's back is black and the female's, grey.

One more treat. Across the river, standing out against a background of emerging green vegetation, was a large bird with marbled black and brown cryptic plumage and a long bill. It was a woodcock, a bird rarely seen in the open.

We decided to end the day on this high. We were all soaking wet and more than ready for the hot baths and good meal we knew would be waiting for us back at Malham Tarn. Conditions had been miserable – and yet, as we climbed aboard the waiting mini-bus, we shared an exhilaration peculiar to birdwatchers, and which cannot be explained.

Perhaps the same E. M. Nicholson once walked in the wet down Wharfedale, listening, like us, to tuneful April songsters singing in the rain. He wrote in his book, *The Art of Birdwatching*, 'For those who practise it, birdwatching is not only a sport and a science, but also something near a religion, and after all its externals have been inventoried, the essence remains – incommunicable.'

The Brambling

Clumber Park, Nottinghamshire

It was already mid-April. Time to be looking for summer migrants. We took a trip to Clumber.

Clumber Park is north of Nottingham in the area known as 'The Dukeries'. It was created by the enclosing of some 3,000 acres of Sherwood Forest in 1707. 'For the use of Queen Anne,' declared the Duke of Newcastle. Timber was in high demand for building ships for the British Navy and many fine trees were felled. But the oaks of Clumber were saved. The woodland of Newstead Abbey and Thoresby Hall, two more 'stately homes', survived. The Dukes halted the fullscale destruction of the Forest, although only fragments remain today.

In Robin Hood's day, Sherwood Forest had occupied one-fifth of the whole area of Nottinghamshire. Villagers were permitted to graze their pigs under its trees, but the grazing of sheep and goats was forbidden. Bows and arrows were banned. Only the King was allowed to hunt. Punishments for killing the king's deer were severe. 'Trespassers against the venison' warranted heavy fines or imprisonment – or worse. Accused men fled and joined the growing band of outlaws.

The *Anglo-Saxon Chronicle* records in verse the hunting enthusiasm of the Norman Conqueror: 'He set apart a vast deer preserve and imposed laws concerning it. Whoever slew a hart or hind was to be blinded. He forbade the killing of boars/Even as the killing of harts. For he loved the stags so dearly/As though he had been their father. Hares also, he decreed should go unmolested. The rich complained and the poor lamented.'

Today the ancient woodland of Clumber, now in the safe keeping of the National Trust, is still rich in bird life and the lake supports wildfowl. It is a good place to listen for newly arriving summer migrants.

We stood beneath the trees – and heard our first chiffchaff of the year: 'Chiff-chaff-chiff-chaff-chiff-*chiff*-chaff.'

As we had hoped, swallows, house martins and sand martins zipped back and forth over the lake, fly-catching, or skimming low to sip, their beaks cutting a line across the still surface of the water.

Willow warblers sang meandering cadences from the trees and a vehement sedge warbler vocalised from a reedbed, letting us know that once again they had safely survived the perilous crossing of arid desert and squally sea.

Satisfied, I began to notice other birds, the all-the-year-round residents. Nuthatches flicked over old leaves in search of insects. A silver and tawny treecreeper spiralled up a tree trunk, probing for beetle larvae with its long thin bill; it dropped down to the roots of the next tree – and edged its way up once more. Jays strutted through a clearing, beak-prodding the ground for green shoots of acorns buried earlier.

The mechanical drumming of a lesser spotted woodpecker raining blows at a branch with its bill reverberated across the park; a strange territorial 'song'.

Tits of several kinds flitted and called tantalisingly: great, blue, coal, marsh and long-tailed. Blackbirds hopped – and paused, heads to one side, then cocked their tails and took off with much commotion to sing full-throatedly from the treetops. Cream-buff willow/chiffs teased: now *which* species is it with the darker legs?

Fat sticky horsechestnut buds; coal-black ash buds with green flower clusters in pairs on the branches; reddish-brown oak buds splitting open to reveal tiny glossy yellow-green leaves: trees were coming to life again after the long winter

Only two months before, the woods were quiet, berries and nuts nearly all gone, seed stocks depleted, insect life sparse. Hunger and the bitter cold would have reduced bird numbers and driven species to flock in the open fields. Now food was plentiful again – and the woods full of song.

We walked along paths beside the lake. Canada geese grazed, stretched their long necks, honked, and grazed again. More birds: pied wagtail, wood pigeon, crow, dunnock, kestrel . . .

Over the footbridge, past Five Thorns Plantation, through Tank Wood and across the weir which splashes down into the River Poulter. Great crested grebe, mallard, tufted duck, coot . . .

We reached Ash Hill Wood. On the branch of a tall pine was a colourful small bird. A splendid male brambling in handsome spring plumage, rich orange, white and glossy black.

But what was a *brambling* doing here? Bramblings are not resident birds – or summer visitors. Bramblings are winter immigrants, normally visiting Britain in rather small numbers each year – but occasionally irrupting in thousands if continental beechmast crops fail. Seldom do they spend successive winters in the same place, but follow the beechmast supply, often in the company of chaffinches.

'A splendid male brambling.'

47

The brambling in the pine tree was on its way back to its breeding grounds in birch woods or conifer forests – where insect populations peak during the short summer season in the far north of Europe. Drab tips of feathers had abraded to expose the bright colours beneath: orange throat, orange chest, jet-black head, white wing bars, bold white rump patch. It was time for this spectacularly handsome winter bird to be gone.

When Bitterns Boom

Leighton Moss, Lancashire

Spring is when the bittern booms. To hear it we travelled to Leighton Moss, that wonderful reserve belonging to the Royal Society for the Protection of Birds close to the shore of Morecambe Bay.

We went first to the Visitor Centre, an old longhouse barn built of locally quarried limestone and slate, to check up on 'new arrivals' – summer migrants flying in. Blackcap, whitethroat and grasshopper warbler had been sighted. Waders were still passing through: spotted redshank, whimbrel, bar-tailed godwit . . . And a marsh harrier was 'about'.

As members of the RSPB the reserve was ours for free; non-members were purchasing permits from 'reception' to gain admittance. So off we set, full of hope, along the wooded path towards the hides.

Wood anemones and celandines studded the damp ground of hazel and alder carr; and clumps of kingcups, a first bluebell and the tiny barren strawberry flower. Graceful spikes of lords-and-ladies pushed up through the earth below white-blossomed blackthorn. Willow warblers sang their delicate down-scale song-phrase and a chiffchaff joined in with its own persistent repetitive notes from the topmost branch of a silver birch.

We only had to wait for five minutes for the first booooooom . . . and a second . . . and a third. A deep, slow, resonant bullish sound; remarkably far-carrying. (The bittern's scientific first name is *Botaurus: bos* = ox, *taurus* = bull).

A hundred years ago, we could have journeyed the length and breadth of Britain to hear the booming of the bittern, but in vain; for the bittern, once common, and 'esteemed a better dish than heron', had become extinct. The last recorded nest with eggs to be found was in Norfolk, in 1868. The Rev C. A. Johns wrote six years earlier, in 1862, 'Of late years, so unusual has the occurrence become of Bitterns breeding in this country, that the discovery of an egg in Norfolk has been thought worthy of being recorded in the transactions of the Linnean Society . . . Stuffed specimens are, however, to be seen in most collections where its form and plumage may be studied . . .'

Land drainage was destroying bittern habitat, but perhaps 'stuffed specimens' and its desirability as an 'esteemed dish' had also a little to do with the bird's disappearance?

But, happily, recolonisation of East Anglia from the continent began at the beginning of this century. And in the 1940s male bitterns were heard booming once again at Leighton Moss. The Royal Society for the Protection of Birds has a genius for encouraging new species into its reserves, making them feel welcome. Reedbeds were extended, water levels regulated, dykes trimmed, pools excavated, scrub kept at bay and willows coppiced. Bittern numbers fluctuate from year to year and a severe winter hits them hard. The British population stands at under forty pairs; up to a dozen pairs breed at Leighton Moss.

We left the trees and walked now between high stands of *phragmites* and reedmace, pausing at a reed screen positioned to hide us from sight. We peeped through the purpose-made hole on to a long dyke and waited hopefully . . . bearded reedling? water rail? bittern? Perhaps an otter? But it was a moorhen that stepped out of the reeds and into the water, flirting its white tail, dipping its head, pecking at the surface with its bright red beak.

From West Hide and from Grizedale Hide we looked through slit windows on to extensive pools. A breeding colony of blackheaded gulls squabbled noisily on their chosen island. Greylag geese grazed at the grassy edge. A coot sat fidgeting on a bulky nest construction, flicking stems out of the way, pushing a twig into position. On a wooden 'loafing platform' sited in the middle of the water a mallard pair snoozed. Through binoculars we recognised shoveler, teal, pochard and tufted duck, all of which breed in the pools. And a shelduck flew in to splash-land.

Two of us decided to walk along the road which led to the public causeway and another, even larger, pool. Close by are woods where, so we were told, there would be a chance of seeing red squirrels.

Retracing our steps, we passed the reed screen once more and I gave a cursory glance through the hole. What I saw, I just couldn't believe! At the far end a *bittern* stood – just as it does in all the books, just as it does in all those television nature films: in bizarre 'bittern-stance'. Its golden plumage barred and streaked with shades of brown and black, its neck extended, its thick, deep-yellow beak pointed skywards, the close-together eyes glassy bright, it stood there on green legs, a large stocky bird, richly coloured – and I knew that this was a once-in-a-lifetime moment.

I nudged my companion. Then reached for my camera. It was too far away for me to get an 'Eric Hosking' but at least I'd possess a 'habitat shot'. It stood there, motionless, and I was amazed at my luck; it is very rare indeed to see a bittern in the open like this, and in daytime.

A small party of birdwatchers rounded a bend in the path fifty yards away and I beckoned them to hurry. But before they could reach the screen, the bittern had stepped, heron-like, slow, deliberate, into the dyke, and across to the other side. With its neck retracted, 'shoulders' hunched, it entered the reedbed, then turned and, passing through the reeds, crossed again. Deeper into the reedbed it went, its cryptic plumage merging with the long, thin, creamy-buff, feathery-topped reedstalks – and disappeared from view.

I remembered two previous springs when, at Minsmere and at Titchwell Marsh, I had enjoyed glimpses of a bittern in flight, briefly, above the reeds: owl-like on rounded wings, legs trailing. At Cley Marshes, I've heard booming, but the bird tantalisingly remained hidden.

There were more highlights that lovely April day. A singing blackcap; a peachy-breasted whinchat; a very spruce wheatear; and swallows and sand martins zipping over the water.

Reed warblers interspersed silvery, repetitive notes with chattering churrs in territorial song and a sedge warbler agitated vociferously from the willow carr. And bittern booming followed us at intervals all day. Evocative sounds of spring.

Kite Country
A Valley in Mid-Wales

We had come in search of raptors and we saw our first after only five minutes of walking. That augured well for the day. A second – and a third – appeared. Buzzards. With great rounded wings, spectacularly patterned pale and dark beneath, they circled effortlessly. Then down swooped a sparrowhawk, smaller, more uniform, feathers of long tail closed.

As it disappeared into the overhanging sessile oakwood, a large and heavy corvine flew across, croaking fruitily. A raven. Not a raptor, but another bird typical of wild Wales.

The sun shone gloriously, the sky was a brilliant blue, the valley in all its spring beauty lured us on. Round another bend – and we were in luck.

It was a red kite that sailed above us now. In these superb light conditions, its deeply forked tail glowed a rich chestnut. Bold white patches adorned the under-sides of its wings and the head appeared white also.

We stood there a long time watching, heads tipped back, neck muscles beginning to ache. If only someone would invent a lubricating oil for birdwatchers . . .

Many years before we had looked for red kites, on a spring camping holiday in the valley of the River Tywi. At the Dinas Reserve we followed the nature trail; a board walk steered us over the boggy bits. Blossom on blackthorn and great banks of bluebells. Wood warblers, chiffchaffs and blackcaps. We picnicked by a pool teeming with tadpoles which the children caught in cupped hands, then released back again.

Each stone on the bank concealed an ant nursery. We felt like gods as we surveyed the distraught insects' frantic efforts to remove precious eggs from sight. We took pity and gently replaced their roofs.

Beetles of every imaginable hue scurried through the grass, mobile jewels. Huge black slugs slid out of curling bracken, delighting the children who wanted to take them home for pets. Goose-grass chasings and a barefoot splashing through a ford, shoes and socks in hand; the skimming and twittering of swallows as they hawked for gnats; grey wagtails flitting from stone to stone in the sparkling waters of the Tywi; a common sandpiper fluting from the far bank. But no red kite.

'Not a good year,' said the Warden.

'It's the new dam, see. They don't like it,' confided a farmer.

'I'm so used to them, you know, don't notice them any more,' laughed the milkman back at the camp site.

We left, defeated. No red kite – until today.

'The children caught tadpoles in cupped hands.'

'The kite swept across the valley.'

We watched as the kite swept across the valley, ascending so high that it was just a speck in the distance, and then swooping gracefully over the horizon, to appear again from behind the next hill.

The female could be incubating eggs in a stick-nest; built high in the tree, the same nest is often used year after year. A 'rubbish heap' of a nest, scraps, grass, wool, rags, paper, string and sheep's wool – stuffed among the sticks. Both birds help in the building; after, the female broods and the male hunts for food.

The red kite cruised out of sight. It was time to take an interest in the wildlife at a lower level in this spectacular valley.

A common lizard struggled through long grass. Bumble bees buzzed. Pale primroses grew on the banks, and mauve violets. Polypody fern flourished in damp crevices . . . yellow celandines besides a stream . . . small tortoiseshell butterflies wafted past . . .

Delightful lambs dotted the fresh green of the valley. Snowy-white and jet black lambs, they suckled vigorously with much ecstatic tail-wagging; bleated, chased each other up and down the slopes, got lost, and again bothered their patient, plodding mothers.

Nature Conservancy Regional Officers have been studying the red kite's food requirements for many years. They examine abandoned nests for prey remains, dissect pellets and talk frequently to local shepherds. Not one piece of evidence has ever come to light to suggest that red kites attack *live* sheep or lambs. It is only carcases of the larger mammals that kites are interested in and help to remove. 'A benign function,' say the researchers.

Live prey includes small mammals, birds (mostly young jackdaws, crows, pigeons and gulls), earthworms and insects. Caught after a spectacular downward stoop from a great height – or, alternatively, after beating low over the terrain to drop with a sudden pounce – the prey is eaten sometimes in flight, sometimes on the ground.

It has taken eighty years for the red kite to recover from near-extinction at the end of the last century when numbers were down to four pairs in a remote part of Wales. Yet in medieval times it was an abundant bird, a useful scavenger in the streets of towns. Later, in Victorian times, birds of prey were persecuted by gamekeepers, by taxidermists and by egg collectors. Fortunately a small group of folk banded together determined to save the bird and the rescue operation began.

Nowadays there is widespread public sympathy. People are prepared to donate money to pay for protection. The Royal Society for the Protection of Birds organises a round-the-clock watch of nests at breeding times, using highly sophisticated electronic equipment. Courts inflict heavy fines on egg thieves. Present-day gamekeepers are tolerant and helpful.

Why, in spite of all these factors, has an increase in population taken so long to achieve? The climate may be to blame, say the experts, continental kites, in warmer conditions, enjoy a higher rate of breeding success. Nevertheless the future of the red kite looks secure, numbering around forty-eight pairs in recent years.

Now we were approaching a steep ravine. We scrambled up the track and found ourselves beside the inevitable little mountain railway. When next the red kite appeared, it sailed below us, allowing us views from above of its long dark wings, streaky red body, red notched tail.

Two acrobatic ravens displayed over our heads. Glossy blue-black, heavily built, they twisted and turned in unison, deep croaks echoing back from the walls of the ravine.

'Buzzard,' shouted someone, 'flying from left to right.' 'Another kite on the horizon,' called someone else. We followed with our binocs the pointing fingers. A 'birdwatcher's neck' in the morning would be a small price to pay.

Dorset Weekend

Portland Bill

Any birdwatcher worth the pinch of salt he always carries in his pocket to sprinkle on the bird's tail, yearns to be on some jutting peninsula at spring migration time. The choice of the Leicestershire and Rutland Ornithological Society this time was Portland Bill, in Dorset. We set off at 4.30am. In the east the sky was streaked yellow and purple. The first birds were waking; the dawn chorus began.

Kestrels hovered at regular intervals down our motorway route. We ate our breakfast in a red-legged partridge patch. By nine o'clock we had reached Portland's furthest point. The peninsula projects a good five miles out into the Channel from the Dorset coastline. It is the first spit of land visible to incoming birds after a considerable sea crossing.

The weather was cold, grey and misty. Birds would be dropping down in relief in such 'fall' conditions. They would be in no hurry to move on. Whilst they rested and fed and waited for the skies to clear, we could enjoy their presence.

So it was. In every bush fluttered tired passerines: wheatears, chiffchaffs, whitethroats, whinchats, willow warblers and linnets.

Portland is almost an island, a great hump of limestone linked to the mainland by the shingle stretch of Chesil Beach. Two-thirds of the hump is quite densely populated, scarred by quarries and dominated by dockland. The remaining third includes the Bill. It is part farmland. But the slopes are grassy, and thickets of brambles, stands of alexander with dark, shiny green leaves, clumps of elder and the Japanese spindle, offer shelter to migrating birds.

They were still flying in. We stood on the cliff top to welcome them, swallows and house martins, meadow pipits and skylarks. High fences around Admiralty installations gave good views as the birds perched briefly on the wires, taking their bearings. A corn bunting was singing halfway up a pylon, short bursts of jangling notes. The weather was clearing, the mist dispersing, the sun began to peep out.

A whinchat paused on the path ahead with the lighthouse as background: a

handsome male in summer plumage, prominent eyestripe, apricot-coloured breast,
pure white markings on tail and wing – so
bright it looked against the brown mud
surround.

A little owl, pretending to be just another
stone on a heap of stones; we could so easily
have missed him if he hadn't swivelled his
head to peer in our direction at just the right
moment.

From a drystone wall inland, redstarts
darted, like orange flames, tail feathers
fanned and quivering. They were catching
insects, shuttling back and forth, storing
energy for the next phase of their long
journey to breeding grounds. Looking along
that wall, I not only had four redstarts in

A little owl

full view in my binoculars, but three cuckoos as well: it was *that* sort of a day.
The cuckoos were resting, half-hidden by brambles. Long white-spotted tails
and barred breasts identified them; then they 'cuckoo'ed gently.

A hundred yards away, a woolly-capped, bearded, anoraked giant was
waving his telescope excitedly in the air. People were hurrying, binoculars
bouncing on chests. They kept carefully to the paths and did not short-cut
across the farmer's fields.

'Golden oriole!'

There had been oriole rumours circulating earlier. We had taken them
with the aforementioned pinch of salt. But here, unmistakably, it was. In full
golden view. Thrush-sized, it perched on a bank. Suddenly it flew – a streak
of brilliant yellow.

Golden orioles in their nesting sites are elusive, impossible to see in the
shimmering canopy of green-gold sunlit leaves. But, once, I heard their song,
a whistling with a magical, far-carrying clarinet quality: 'Oooooo-weooo,'
Hammock-nests, lined with flowery grassheads, are slung high up out of sight
across forked branches.

Now the secretive whistler with the woodwind song was revealed. Exotica
on an open headland; a black and yellow bird with a poetical name on the
windy top of Portland Bill in early May.

Radipole Lake, Weymouth

There must be very few bird reserves situated only a few minutes' walk from
the centre of a town which turn out to be as rewarding as Radipole Lake,
another RSPB reserve. That evening, after dinner at our hotel, we walked
along its reed-lined paths which lead past dykes and inter-connecting
lagoons. We could smell the salty tang of sea air less than a mile away, and
we could hear the mewing of gulls. The evening air was cool. The reedbed

bird chorus was at its peak, a last clamorous burst before the light grew dim.

Reed and sedge warblers were the dominant songsters. Warblings, chatterings, churrings; they sang unseen. We identified the 'chi-chi-chitty' of the reed bunting and the 'pching, pching' of a bearded reedling. Tell-tale movements in the reeds betrayed bird passage.

Suddenly an astonishingly loud eruption of staccato notes exploded from willow scrub at the edge of the path. Only to cease as abruptly as it had begun. 'Cetti's,' the word went round.

The spread of the Cetti's warbler across the south of England in recent years is well documented. With such a distinctive song it can scarcely be missed. It moved northward through France from the Mediterranean coast and was recorded for the first time in Britain at a site in Hampshire, in March 1961. Breeding was confirmed ten years later in the Kent marshes, and it has been increasing in numbers and colonising more reedbeds in the years since.

Thousands of migrating martins and swallows were settling to roost, with a great deal of twittering, in the reeds. The song chorus died down. A female mallard quacked sleepily and was silent. Just one wideawake sedge warbler sang solo as stars began to twinkle in the darkening night sky.

Studland Heath

Studland Heath is an area of heathland which stretches away towards Poole Harbour and the sea. There were rumours that a pied-billed grebe had settled on 'Little Sea', a freshwater lagoon cut off from the coast by the gradual build-up of sand dunes. On the Sunday of our Dorset weekend we decided to go in search.

The sun blazed down as we followed narrow paths through the ling. Gorse was spectacular, a brilliant yellow. Past silver birches and Scots pines we walked to reach the small hide at the edge of Little Sea,

But Little Sea was empty of bird life. We waited hopefully. The odd moorhen appeared; and a couple of mallards. A roe deer came down into reeds opposite to munch at green stuff. Once, even, a *grebe* swam across. Try as we might, we could not persuade ourselves that its dabchick-bill was pied.

Less than a dozen pied-billed grebes have been recorded in Britain. The birds migrate from South American wintering quarters to North American breeding grounds. Very occasionally one ends up on the wrong side of the Atlantic.

It sounds altogether a very odd bird. 'Listen for its slurred, gulping notes, increasing in speed and loudness,' reads one report, 'notes which are often drawn out into a long whistling finale.' It has some curious habits. It swims close to the bank and squats in the shallows where it makes 'vigorous paddling movements' with its feet to stir up small fish.

We were looking for a bird in brown and white breeding plumage. In summer its bill is short and thick, bluish-white in colour and banded across the middle with black. Distinctive white orbital rings circle its red eyes, and the throat is black.

More folk arrived at the hide and we relinquished our places. No black-striped bill had we seen, or slurring gulps heard. But Dartford warblers were next on the 'list'. Studland Heath is one of the few localities where this rare and elusive bird builds its nest – in heather or gorse. We kept to the paths, being specially careful where we put our feet; ground nesting species are at their most vulnerable in spring.

Dartford warbler numbers fluctuate dramatically. Severe fires, drought, recent ploughing of the heathland edges, increasing throngs of holiday-makers (and careless birdwatchers?) are probably all detrimental factors. In a hard winter the population plummets, for it is a non-migratory species, an insectivore, unable to supplement its diet with fruit and berries. In Britain, at the very edge of its breeding range, it is living under less than optimum conditions.

Stonechats, perched on gorse twig songposts, 'chack'ed at us. 'To find Dartford warblers, search in areas where stonechats are in evidence,' say the old hands.

The weather was fine and bright. 'In fine bright weather the Dartford warbler is more inclined to show itself.' But – 'The chances of seeing one without being shown by the Warden are nil,' warns John Gooders in his book, *Where to Watch Birds.*

We soon gave up the hunt. It was hot. We were tired. A sandy bank looked a good place for a snooze. We stepped carefully around a patch of particularly scratchy heather – just as a small reptile emerged from beneath: a lizard, about eight inches long, patterned with blotches and white-centred rings which ran down its grass-green horny back and tail.

Our herpetologist identified it. It was the rarest of all British lizards: a sand lizard. 'A male. And he's in his seldom seen breeding skin.'

After hibernating through the winter months, a male sand lizard wakes up and sheds his old brown skin for a new green one which the duller female finds attractive. After mating, she lays eggs – sand lizards are the only British oviparous lizard. The other two British lizard species, the slow worm and the common lizard, are viviparous – the young grow inside the mother and are born without egg shells.

Our sand lizard, resembling a green mini-monster from prehistoric times, scrambled over the twiggy heather. His Latin name is *Lacerta agilis* but he wasn't particularly 'agile' that day. Perhaps he was still sleepy, or had just indulged in a stultifying beetle meal.

We didn't attempt to touch him for a lizard can easily lose its tail at the defensive snapping point. The tail would grow again – but the join would spoil its beauty. Not only that; we would be breaking the law if we 'interfered' with him in any way; the sand lizard is considered rare enough to have been designated a 'protected species' (Wildlife and Countryside Act, 1981).

Now he was lost from view. Sand lizards spend most of their time in burrows underground; we had been very lucky. Not many ticks had been added to our bird list, but we'd earned a very fine tick for our lizard list!

Red-Necked Phalarope

Cley Marshes, Norfolk

It was in May that I met her, on a return visit to Cley. The Amazon of the bird world – the ultimate in hen's lib.

With the blessing of the Norfolk Naturalists' Trust and with special permits in our pockets (obtainable from the Visitors' Centre) we had walked along their famous bank from road to sea. Channels and saltmarsh, reedbeds and pools, shingle and foreshore.

Sedge warblers sang exulting in the willow scrub. From hides we watched skimming house martins, skulking moorhens, skidding coots, a hovering kestrel, soaring skylarks, mud-probing greenshanks and fast-pecking black-bellied dunlins.

Bearded reedlings sallied forth obligingly from the reeds. One graceful avocet, in positively dazzling black and white plumage, swept for ragworms with long, upward-curving bill. Fishing terns hovered and flitted and splashed. Showing off his cinnamon-red summer colours was a bar-tailed godwit, another 'passage wader' passing through.

A ringed plover looked trustingly up from her nest on the shingle, so close to the path, and did not stir as we filed quietly by. Oystercatchers preened on an island. A marsh harrier flapped slow-stately past. Lapwings tumbled, twisted, plunged and shrilled, 'Pee-wit'. And a bittern boomed. It really did. A deep, far-carrying, resonant booooooom.

In fact, the Cley marshes were alive with springtime sound; the bosun pipe's whistle of the oystercatcher, the 'teu-hu-hu' of the redshank, the high-pitched, squeaky 'seep-seep-seep' of the common sandpiper, the liquid yelping of the avocet, the harsh scolding of black-headed gulls, the screeching of terns.

It wasn't until the fourth hide was reached that I met that extraordinary bird, the red-necked phalarope. I watched, entranced, through the hide opening as it bobbed like a cork below me; light and buoyant, swimming in gentle circles, spinning, pecking at surface morsels. Only seven inches long, and exquisite.

Floating there, it could have been a bathtoy duck, daintily hand-painted by some artistic genius, plaything of a princess, if it weren't for its air of fragility, and slim – needle-slim – bill. Buoyant as a duck, slender as a sandpiper, small as a dunlin. Snowy-white throat and belly, orange-red cheeks and collar, and the rest of the plumage a mosaic of slate-grey, blue and brown.

I didn't know about phalaropes at the time. I was quite ignorant of their lifestyle and topsy-turvy habits. I flipped through the pages of my field guide. Red-necked phalarope. Summer plumage.

'That's odd,' I thought. 'They've got their symbols muddled up. The female in these drawings looks brighter than the male. Surely, if there is any differentiation at all between the sexes, the hen bird is always duller than the cock.'

I confided my problem to my neighbour on the hide bench. 'Not so,' he whispered. 'They're amazing birds, phalaropes. Reversal of roles. The female of the species *is* the brightest.'

It seems that, quite contrarily, it is *she* who courts the male, and *he* who rears the chicks.

'Only other bird I know as dotty as that is . . . the dotterel,' declared my hide companion.

Well, well, well!

Red-necked phalarope

Most waders *share* the egg-and-chick-minding duties. Male and female avocet, dunlin, redshank, common sandpiper, curlew, turnstone, black-tailed godwit, golden plover, ringed plover and little ringed plover – each (according to the encyclopaedic *Birds of the Western Palearctic*) normally plays a more or less equal part in the incubation and brooding of the young.

The macho ruff is an exception. In spring he dons his curious plumage: long ear tufts, and dramatic barred, streaked, blobbed or plain ruff-collar. 'Lekking' ruffs meet to display on arenas. They show off shamefully to the females (reeves). They 'wing-tremble' and 'flutter-jump' and 'strut-walk' and 'bill-thrust' and raise their huge loose ruffs. Full of self-importance, they take no part in parental duties. The females cope alone.

It is quite the opposite with the red-necked phalarope. The *female* entices the male on to her territory with a wing-whirring display flight to advertise her presence. Then she and her mate build a number of scrapes near shallow freshwater pools or streams in the wild open country of their northerly breeding grounds.

The female makes the final choice and lays her eggs in the shallow depression. After which she goes off to join the other hens, leaving the male to incubate the eggs alone and to lead the chicks away from the scrape to a safe and secret hideaway. Protectively he 'mothers' them.

Phalaropes are unconventional in other ways too. They spend their time far out on warm seas once the short northern summer is over. Expert swimmers, they only occasionally venture ashore on migratory passage. Sometimes they get blown off course by exceptionally strong winds – to thrill birdwatchers by their apparent 'tameness' and exquisite plumage; to spin on the spot in circles; and to dab at the water surface for invertebrate food.

Down flew a handsome drake, on to the muddy bank beneath the hide. 'Mallard. Splendid specimen,' commented my chauvinist companion. 'None of this sex role reversal nonsense. Female duller. And domesticated. Male wears the trousers. Shows who's boss. As it should be . . .'

Songbird Census
Gibraltar Point, near Skegness, Lincolnshire

I filled the freezer with pizzas, pies and raspberry ripple ice-cream and caught the train to Skegness. The family could quite well manage without me for two days.

On arrival at Gibraltar Point Field Station, I tracked down my single bedroom and, as one does, went immediately to the window and peered out. Two bright goldfinches and one red-breasted linnet were just standing there. My first reaction was to rush out and proclaim the news at the top of my voice. Fortunately, as it turned out, shyness got the better of me and I stayed put.

Very fortunately, for goldfinches and linnets, I soon discovered, happened to be two of the reserve's commonest species and it would have been akin to rushing out to tell my neighbours back home that I had just seen a sparrow in the yard.

Gibraltar Point is a splendid nature reserve, managed by the Lincolnshire and South Humberside Trust. It contains almost every type of habitat a discerning bird could wish for: a scrub full of buckthorn, sand dunes held secure with marram grass, saltmarsh rich with colonising plants, lush woodland and pasture near old farm buildings, shingle spits and winding muddy creeks. There is even a bird-enticing mere built especially for them, with islands, and high banks to keep out unwanted humans.

The field station consists of a modern annexe built on to the old coastguard station. As is the way of coastguard stations, it once had waves lapping at its doorstep. But, over the last hundred years, acres of 'accumulated land' have built up and it is now a good trek from station to sea.

Year by year the reserve is increasing in size and more sand and silt is washed in. One day the residents of Skegness may arrive with their buckets and spades and wheelbarrows to demand back their sand, but meanwhile the owners of Gibraltar Point are sitting pretty.

I joined other escaping mums – and dads and younger folk and older folk too. Our tutor was to introduce us to 'fieldwork'. Fieldwork, Ted Smith explained, concerned looking for birds, and listening; recording and making notes.

Bullfinch

Looking for distinguishing marks – the upturned bill of the bar-tailed godwit, the chocolate brown head and white cheek with its black spot of the tree sparrow, the double white wingbar of the chaffinch, the square patch of white above the bullfinch's tail, the grey head and bandit mask of the jackdaw, the bold eyestripe of the sedge warbler.

And *listening* to songsters in a month when song is at its peak.

Birdsong has always fascinated people. It is a favourite subject for poets. They speak of 'mirth', 'melody', 'merriment' and 'madrigals'. 'And ilka bird sang of its love,' wrote Burns. 'My heart is like a singing bird,' rhapsodised Rossetti. 'We'd be as happy as the birds in spring,' sighed Blake. 'Then sing, ye Birds, sing, sing a joyous song!' commanded Wordsworth. And Chaucer heard 'the voice of angels in their harmony.'

But scientists think differently. They speak of 'vocal belligerence', 'defensive territorial activity', 'ritualistic aggression' and 'matrimonial advertisement'. They analyse 'frequency', measure 'intensity', speculate on 'motivation', design 'sound spectrums' and discuss 'seasonal variation'.

'Vocal belligerence?'

We were given maps of the reserve and told how to census the songsters by marking the grid position of each singing bird. I hid myself away in the long grass at the edge of the wood near Sykes Farm. A whitethroat's scratchy effort . . . wren chittering . . . lesser whitethroat rattle . . . two cheerfully competing chaffinches . . . catchy phrases of a song thrush . . . silvery fluting of a blackbird . . . the complex pattern of dunnock notes . . . harsh chatter of magpie . . .

I noted the position of each male's songpost on the map and speculated on territory. A census taken in this way each year follows the fortunes of individual species; it is an indicator of population change, and perhaps of changes in the environment.

On Sunday I was up at 6am. Ringed plovers pattered at the water's edge of a muddy creek and a whimbrel whistled as it flew overhead. Little terns fished out at sea; I could hear their squabblings as I walked across the sandhills. Small silver-white sanderling sped across the wet sand following the line of the waves, surface-snatching, 'twinkling' along the beach.

I followed a path to the hide by the mere. Settling myself on the wooden bench I peered through the open slit. What birds would be about? On the smallest of the islands a shelduck couple cosily cuddled. A party of skylarks were taking a breather from their incessant high-rise singing to indulge in an early-morning splashing. I trained my binoculars on the reeds closest to the hide; an up-and-down bobbing movement had caught my eye. It was a jack snipe, bobbing rhythmically on green legs in the shallow water.

A redshank swept its bill through soft patches of wet mud and breakfasted on tiny insects, shrimps and wriggling worms. Grey herons contorted to strange shapes as they stretched long necks and peered into the shallows. Two fox cubs romped playfully on the bank.

Best of all, a kingfisher, black against the red sun, alighted on a post at the far end. Then it whirred the length of the mere to perch on a whitened branch below me. There it posed, alert, head jerking; coral red legs; a metallic sheen to its feathers: bright blue and green, white and orange.

Suddenly it plunged into the water and, a swift streak, returned to its perch with a silver fish in its dagger-bill. Casually it beat the fish into stillness on the branch and swallowed it in one gulp. Three times it did this, then, satisfied, it flashed – electric blue – into the reeds and disappeared.

Sunday afternoon arrived far too soon. We swopped experiences for the last time. Tiny vivid-green hairstreak butterflies in abundance. An orangetip butterfly sighting – a 'first' for the reserve. A grass snake swimming obligingly from island to bank in full view of watchers. Striped snail shells lying shattered at a song thrush anvil. A skylark's nest in a rabbit burrow with four tiny brown-blotched eggs.

But no-one could better my kingfisher.

Birds – and all that Jizz

Goyt, Derbyshire

We were high above Goyt Valley on a sombre millstone grit moor 'which,' said the guide book, 'can be tackled by anyone sound in wind and limb.'

'Go-back, go-back,' something was bossing rather rudely. I looked questioningly at my neighbour. 'Red grouse,' he said. We gazed long and hard but could not spot the unwelcoming creature, our first true upland species. Red grouse eat heather shoots. This one was lying low in a heathery jungle.

'Sure to see some later,' said Dave. Younger folk had grown impatient and were now signalling frantically a hundred yards ahead. On a stone wall perched a black bird with a white bib: it was a ring ouzel, a bird of mountain and moorland. A female appeared, brown; her bib (gorget) was buff. So they were probably breeding.

We walked on, jumping over trickles of water, squelching through soggy bits, scrambling over dry stands of heather, bouncing off spongy peat, clambering around rocky outcrops.

A curlew flew over, its call a haunting lament: 'Corli, corli'. No moorland is complete without its curlew overhead. Meadow pipits, commonest of upland birds, negotiated undulating flightpaths over white tufts of cotton grass. Ubiquitous skylarks sang madly in the blue above. Swifts screeched, soared and swept after midges.

There was no need for anyone to consult his pocket field guide. Someone always 'knew', the advantage of birdwatching in a group. I felt I had joined an Out-in-the-Open University crash course in bird identification.

We picnicked on the leeward side of a wall. Curious gritstone ewes with speckled black faces came to watch, lambs frisking at their sides. Our meal was constantly interrupted by sightings. A pair of black-headed, white-collared reed buntings preened on bracken fronds, their white-edged tails constantly flickering. A whinchat perched, first atop a tussock – 'Tic, tic, tic, tu-tic' – then it flew up on to a boulder to continue its scolding. Swallows skimmed low: 'Tsit-tswit-tswit'.

Then a cuckoo flew over. Shallow beats of thin pointed wings – fast and straight – small head, long spotty tail drooping: cuckoo jizz.

Someone recognised a tree pipit – by its jizz. A tree pipit is another nondescript 'little brown job', almost indistinguishable from the meadow pipit except for its remarkable song flight. At first it was just a dot in the valley below, perched on the topmost branch of a lightning-blasted conifer. Suddenly it soared forty feet up into the air, singing as it accelerated, a clear, far-carrying song: 'Tseep, tseep, tseep.'

We watched fascinated as it parachuted down in slow descent, tail fanned, wings tilted upwards. 'See-er, see-er, see-er,' it sang, descending leisurely back to an adjacent tree perch. Without doubt, everyone agreed, this extraordinary display proved it to be a tree pipit. Up it went again, and the whole performance was repeated.

A male wheatear flicked its wings and white-rumped tail from a grey stone wall. Its stance was upright, perky, bold: wheatear jizz. A kestrel hovered above the brow of the hill: very easy kestrel jizz!

Jizz? The characteristic which singles out a species; its idiosyncratic style of flying, perching, feeding, ground-moving, preening, posturing which, once observed in the field, identifies it from the rest.

'There's something about its jizz which makes me think it's a . . .' is a very handy phrase when only a brief glimpse of the bird has been caught.

We walked on, past sessile oaks and bilberry patches, downhill until we reached the valley. Across Goyt Bridge – a pretty little packhorse bridge which was moved from its position further down the valley, stone by stone, by enlightened planners intent on preventing it being 'drowned' when the two new reservoirs were built. Silvery water swirled beneath and we spied grey wagtails on wet boulders in mid-stream. Beautiful yellow and grey birds, they balanced skilfully, long slender tails never ceasing a delicate shivering. There was no mistaking *their* jizz. ('It's a grey wagtail, that's what jizz.')

We were entering woodland and, by the twittering and warbling from oak, ash and pine, were going to see more birds. We stood in the shadows and waited patiently.

Redstarts flicked long chestnut tails and flashed white foreheads as they chased in and out of the branches. We heard the high-pitched squeaks of a goldcrest. A green woodpecker's laughing yaffle call rang out. Willow warblers, chiffchaffs, blue tits and wrens all appeared within sight as we stood there quietly. A female blackbird flew by with a stick in her beak; she was nest building.

Time was passing and now we were approaching the reservoirs, Fernilee and Errwood. People were everywhere, walking, fishing, boating, following nature trails past rhododendron bushes and azalea shrubs. We queued for ice creams and it was time to go.

'But you promised we'd see red grouse,' wailed an insatiable lad.

'Next time!'

It's good that there's always a next time for birds – and all that jizz.

Disappearing Headland

Spurn Head, North Humberside

When I read in my newspaper that Spurn Head could well tumble into the sea at any moment, given a sufficiently powerful gale, I felt I must visit the place quickly before it did so, before great waves breached its narrowness and destroyed it – yet again. So I wrote to the Warden of Spurn Bird Observatory and booked myself in for a night.

Spurn is a long thin peninsula, jutting three-and-a-half miles out from the North Humberside mainland. On one side is a sandy shore and the wide open sea; on the other, the mudflats of the Humber estuary. In spring, the Head is used by migrants, the bulk of birds passing through in April and May. An easterly wind can produce the unusual bird, an off-route 'accidental', an 'overshooter' or 'drifter'. Spurn Head has a reputation for rarities.

On arrival, I was welcomed and shown to my quarters in an ex-War Department bungalow. (The Yorkshire Wildlife Trust bought the peninsula from the Ministry of Defence in 1959.) 'Running hot water and flush loos,' I noted with satisfaction. I had experienced other bird observatories; some were less well-endowed with the amenities of civilised living. I got out my sheet sleeping bag and slipped it between the regulation army blankets on the bed.

Then, before it grew dark, I decided on a quick sprint up to the Narrow Neck, the area most vulnerable in times of storm. I saw tank traps and great banks of boulder clay where the road had been repaired in make-shift fashion after the last perilous night of violent north-easterlies. The peninsula on that occasion had not been breached – quite. But next time?

The long stretch of the spit curved ahead of me. The tide was out and, to my right, vast acres of mud glistened in the light of the low sun, a rich feeding ground for waders. To my left, was sand: sandy beaches and dunes. Blue-green marram grass, white daisies, scarlet pimpernel, pink storksbill, yellow birdsfoot trefoil, silver-veined blue-grey leaves of sea holly; flowers of the seashore speckled the dunes with colour.

But sea buckthorn dominated: the climax plant of Spurn. It spread the length of the long spit, a thorny barrier and shelter for birds. At the Point stood the black and white lighthouse and the coastguard station, silhouetted now, for dusk was falling fast and it had turned chilly. I retraced my steps. Two curlews flew over, calling plaintively, dark against a greying sky.

(top right) Swans on ice; (right) A good cowslip year; (far right) Early purple orchid

'A long thin peninsula.'

Later, after fry-ups in the communal kitchen, everyone gathered in the common room. A driftwood fire blazed in the grate and we sat warming ourselves as the flames leapt. Then the Warden arrived with the Observatory Log Book.

Filling in the log is an evening ritual at all bird observatories. A census of birds sighted each day throughout the year, and kept up for a considerable number of years, is an invaluable source of information to all concerned with the monitoring of bird numbers.

'Divers, grebes, fulmars, shearwaters . . . Cormorants, shags, herons, geese . . . Ducks, buzzards, kestrels . . .'

The youngest visitor, aged about six and dressed ready for bed in pyjamas, helped his father to decipher the jottings in his field notebook and then reported earnestly on the day's tally. 'You can always tell the linnets by their bouncy flight,' he added. It was obvious that he was a Jim Flegg in the making.

The bed was comfortable and I slept like a top. For a short while. It is the early birdwatcher that catches the bird. And even if one wanted to at a bird observatory, one would find it difficult to lie in. Alarms ring, doors slam, taps run, boots reverberate . . . from four o'clock onwards.

I yawned my way back to the Narrow Neck. The tide was high now and waders were feeding at the water's edge. A turnstone in tortoiseshell plumage

Puffins on Bempton Cliff

flicked over stones and pecked smartly at exposed food items. Three more turnstones scooped up sand, pushing with the tops of bills and leaving tiny dark streaks and spattered sand grains which showed where they had dug, excavating for sandhoppers.

Bar-tailed godwits probed deep, skewering with long bills. Dunlin pecked rhythmically and fast, pattering over the mud. A whimbrel sailed over, landed, and showed off its striped crown as it tackled a bivalve. Twelve oystercatchers flew past in a straight follow-my-leader line, piping ecstatically.

It was a glorious sunny morning with very little wind. I took a deep breath and smelt the sea. A sea mist far out kept the lighthouse foghorn blaring. And linnets ('with bouncy flight') were on the move, flying to the end of the Point. I counted as they twittered past. One hundred and twenty, I wrote down in my notebook.

More twittering as small parties of swallows skimmed over the buckthorn, twisting and weaving, blue-black streaks with fine tail streamers.

Someone else was already in possession of the sea-watching hut.

'Sandwich terns,' he called out as I passed. Two white birds with long black shaggy caps, forked tails and black, yellow-tipped beaks zipped eastwards towards the rising sun. A solitary swift flew over, followed by a trickle of house martins. Then an immature gannet came into view away out at sea, a huge bird, still in mottled dark brown plumage.

I strolled on (binoculars always at the ready, afraid of what I might miss) as far as the Wire Dump Heligoland trap. One day this whole area might be an island, a gradually disappearing island. Every two hundred and fifty years throughout the known history of Spurn – and there are apparently records dating from 600AD onwards – the sea wins the battle. The peninsula is breached and the Head vanishes.

Only to rebuild itself again, with sand washed from the boulder clays of Holderness, in the decades to follow. Kings out to claim thrones landed here (Henry IV, Edward IV), ports, towns, monasteries, chapels, lighthouses, hermits have come and gone. At least four Spurns were in existence before the present one.

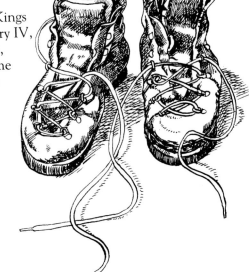

'Boots reverberate.'

Today, with the designation 'moving headland', Spurn Head is scheduled a Site of Special Scientific Interest, worthy of special treatment for its geophysical characteristics as well as for the diversity of its flora and fauna and its value to migratory birds.

In the middle of the nineteenth century when, according to calculations, destruction was again imminent, the canny Victorians strengthened defences. They built timber groynes and constructed chalk banks and patched up breaches as they occurred. Their work has withstood the storms of a hundred years and more. The sea was temporarily thwarted. Now I had reached the remains of one of those chalk banks built by Victorian engineers. A whistling 'Wheet, chack-chack,' I heard. 'Wheatear,' I wrote down in my little book.

Reed buntings, resident birds, chittied away, spring-time spruce and immaculate. The whitethroats' singing was even louder, a monotonous scratchy sound. Their small bodies quivered with the exertion. What other birds breed on Spurn? Meadow pipits and skylarks, redpolls and linnets.

Well-satisfied, and by now very hungry, I walked back to the observatory for breakfast.

Later that morning I was glad I had risen early. Hordes of day trippers began to arrive in their cars. A road runs the length of Spurn Head from the Observatory to the Point and soon the small beaches and dune slopes were filled with the bucket-and-spade brigade.

I gave up being a birdwatcher and succumbed to the delicious trippery feel of sun on my back and sand on my front. But time was running out. The journey home had to be faced. And it looked as if I was going to have to leave without that promised rarity. 'You should have been here the day before yesterday . .' they'd said. Two daus ago a red-spotted bluethroat had thrilled. I had arrived two days too late.

Thinking these thoughts, I approached the observatory complex. Only to find that Barry Spence, the Warden, had sent out a search party for me. A red-breasted flycatcher had been caught in the Garden Heligoland trap. It was a little mouse-brown bird, a female. The white patches on its tail, bristles at the broad base of its bill and big eyes with pale eye rings confirmed the diagnosis. But no 'red breast'; only the male is so adorned.

She had already been measured and weighed, and found smaller and lighter than the pied or spotted flycatchers. Now she was ready for release. With a tiny numbered ring on her leg, she flew off. She was far to the west of her east-European breeding grounds and only the thrid spring red-breasted flycatcher record for Spurn.

I packed my rucksack, signed the visitors' book, left my list of sightings in the common room and said my farewells.

'See you again soon, I hope,' I said. I'd like to return to Spurn whilst it is still there to return to – before the gales of winter win their battle and demolish it yet again.

Urban Reserve

Potteric Carr, near Doncaster, Yorkshire

'Did you see the harrier? Flew over the viaduct, splendid view, hen harrier, male, grey,' he bawled.

'No,' I yelled back, 'missed it. Saw the black tern though.'

Shouting was necessary, for it happened that a high-speed train was rushing by at just that moment on a main line to the east coast.

We were standing in the middle of an amazing nature reserve. It had once been a 'spaghetti-junction' of railway lines, all converging on Doncaster, a couple of miles distant. Some of the branch lines had been closed down in the Beeching fifties. Colliery lines and sidings have shut. But trains still racket by frequently with ear-splitting effect.

Heavy lorries thunder along motorways to the south. Pylons, slag heaps, water towers, workshops, collieries sprawl messily outside the boundaries. Smoke belches from factory complexes on the horizon.

Within the reserve, signals rear above silver birch groves, drains criss-cross, embankments loom, the pumping station emits strange noises, a converted railway hut serves as a field station and a disused marshalling yard sprouts rosebay willow-herb. Derelict railway lines are now covered with earth or ashes and grass-seeded, well disguised as useful paths to lead us through this extraordinary cheek-by-jowl-with-industry urban reserve.

As we walked along the track from the car park on that sparkling May morning, swifts skimmed low over our heads after swarming gnats, dainty white lady's smock swayed in the breeze, and a little owl stared solemnly and unblinkingly at us from the fork of an oak tree. We had been met on arrival (a prior arrangement) by members of the Yorkshire Wildlife Trust.

'It's a jigsaw puzzle of a reserve,' we were told. 'Since 1968 we've been doing our best to piece the fragments into a satisfying whole. For six years we lived under the threat that the M18 could be driven straight through the centre. Fortunately vigorous campaigning stayed the planners but, always, management will be an exercise in compromise.'

We divided into small groups. Each followed a guide; mine knew the place thoroughly for he paid regular visits throughout the year.

'There's always something new to see,' he said, 'and plenty of work to do.'

He led us past the remains of the Young Eea, a copse of blackened and dead trees, planted some 150 years ago, but drowned when the land was inundated with water. Leafless, twigless, they stood stark and straight – a petrified forest – on their island ('eea' meaning island).

'The woodpeckers and treecreepers find good nesting holes in the rotting wood; starlings, tits and kestrels, too.'

We followed along the seeded track. On our left, silver birches full of willow warbler song and redpoll twittering; to our right, willow scrub and a healthy stretch of reedbed. Bearded tits visit, the bittern booms and, by the sound of it, reed warblers were present in abundance.

'There's sedge warblers in there, too,' said our guide. We listened with renewed interest to the chorus. 'We're pleased about the reed warblers: they're at the north-westerly edge of their breeding range here,' he went on. 'It always astonishes me – the *silence* of the reedbeds once the young have hatched. Singing stops as soon as there are youngsters to feed.'

We were beginning to understand why the farsighted Yorkshire Trust had been so keen to acquire Potteric Carr to add to their collection of nature reserves. We were getting an idea of the richness of its segmented habitats, the potential of this city's edge sanctuary. The history of the hundred hectares is as extraordinary as the place itself. Until the eighteenth century, it was largely an impenetrable morass of bog and fen. Several attempts were made at drainage but without success until the 1760s. By the end of that century, engineers had converted a large part of the area to agricultural land. Most of the original marshland flora and fauna disappeared, to be replaced by newly planted trees and hedges.

The Industrial Revolution saw the next dramatic change. Doncaster was soon the second largest railway centre in Britain and lines intersected in all directions. Industry encroached, roads ribboned, and the previously attractive landscape became dreary wasteland as farmers abandoned the small cut-off parcels of arable land as no longer being worth the effort.

Potteric Carr was an eyesore. It would have remained so to this day – but for the unforseen results of subsidence. Seams from Rossington Colliery undermined the whole area between 1960 and 1967. Ground caved in, pools formed, pastures flooded. After two hundred years Potteric Carr was once again an area of extensive marsh with open water. Back came the water violet. Other marsh plants quickly colonised. Aquatic invertebrates returned. In flew the birds. The Yorkshire Wildlife Trust was delighted, and secured the lease from a sympathetic British Rail. Today we were reaping the benefit.

By now we had reached a delectable small pool hidden away in willow trees: Willow Pool. We sat in a hide built from old telegraph poles and railway sleepers and looked out on to banks bright with primroses and cowslips. Last year's reedmace and teasel stood tall, a natural 'dried flower arrangement' decoratively framing our hide-slit view.

A water vole swam vigorously across from a little island, its round face and bright eyes showing above the water. A little grebe, chestnut-cheeked, suddenly dived – and reappeared again close to the furthest bank with a shimmering fish in its beak. Two Canada geese and a pair of tufted duck drifted peacefully in this secret place.

'That's the branch where the kingfisher alights,' pointed out our voluntary warden, 'and yonder, we've put up a nesting box. Starlings, squirrels, kestrels

– they all use our nesting boxes. But we're hoping for long-eared owls in this one.'

We saw two long-eared owls later, fluffing out their feathers. They sat upright and close against the trunk of a tree in a stand of mature woodland which had miraculously survived industrial upheavals. Spring leaves were still new and shiny and satiny. It was catkin time on willow, alder, oak, hazel and silver birch.

'A water vole swam across.'

But first we had visited Decoy Marsh, the site of an early duck decoy built by seventeenth-century Dutch engineers who fancied roast duck on their menu. (The word 'decoy' derives from the Dutch *eende*, meaning 'duck', and *kool* meaning 'cage'.) A tunnel of netting stretched over semi-circular hoops narrowed down to a small catching area. Captive ducks, or a dog, were used to lure the birds into the trap. Catches were well documented at the time and proceeds from sales were distributed to the poor of Doncaster.

We walked along the top bank of a reclaimed tip where lapwing nest. A startled whinchat sprang up and over and disappeared into a hawthorn hedge. Black-headed gulls circled, spiralling skywards in a current of warm air. A delicately graceful turtle dove fanned its tail and purred its soporific summer song – 'Rrroorrrr, rrroorrrrrr' – from the top of an oak tree; a much persecuted bird, it had run the gauntlet of continental guns and arrived safely.

Gorse blossomed gold on magnesium limestone embankments and, with our hearts in our mouths, and the necessary British Rail Permit in our guide's pocket, we crossed the line.

A confusion of flowers, some lime-loving, grow on the strange mix of ballast soils imported for embankment construction: St John's wort, mullein, ground ivy, wild strawberry, silverweed, yellow iris, horse radish, wild mint, purple loosestrife, yellow-wort, meadow cranesbill, evening primrose – and more.

We visited more hides, followed a winding stream, were shown the favourite skulking haunt of a water rail and listened (with no luck) for its 'lilo-emptying' squeal. Finally we sat in the hide open to the general public and looked out over the wide expanse of water at Low Ellers.

In the shallows, 'short-legged wader jobs' paused on migratory passage: ringed plover and dunlin. A heron stood motionless for long minutes before grandmother-footstepping its way: step – freeze – step – freeze – step – freeze – *stab*! Then flew away, slow-flapping wings, neck held in a curving S-shape. On deeper water teal, mallard and great crested grebes bobbed and coots squawked and chased each other noisily. Overhead, swallows and house martins hawked.

Our guide's enthusiasm seems to be shared by all concerned. British Rail are helpful; the Water Authority with its moderate drainage scheme and its new pumping station has promised to keep wildlife in mind when regulating levels; the South Yorkshire County Council gives useful financial assistance; the Manpower Services Commission provides stalwart helpers.

There are plans afoot to extend scrapes and depollute drains. More than 200 species of birds have been sighted on the reserve and over 80 species have bred. The greatest 'catch' of all is the first recorded breeding in Britain of the little bittern.

And all this on the edge of a great industrial city! We left inspired by the example of Potteric Carr. Maybe, we wondered, there are derelict areas, or a few jigsaw puzzle pieces, on the edge of our own city, or within its boundaries which, with a little compromise and a lot of imagination . . .?

In the Shadow of Cooling Towers

Thorpe Marsh, near Doncaster, Yorkshire

In the shadow of the gigantic cooling towers of Thorpe Marsh, North Eastern Region's 1000 MW Coal-fired Power Station, is an exciting area set aside for wildlife.

Thorpe Marsh Reserve was created when quick-witted local naturalists learned of the proposed building of embankments to enclose an extensive ash disposal area. The soil for the embankments was to be dug out from 'ecologically poor' land close by. The potential of such a large excavated area was obvious. Design indented shorelines with sloping shelves and islands, fill it up with water, plant vegetation – and wait for the wildfowl to fly in to the resulting 'dug out' lake.

Consultations took place between the Central Electricity Generating Board, the Yorkshire Wildlife Trust and the South Yorkshire County Council and the proposed scheme for a lake was given the go-ahead.

We wrote to the Trust for a permit to visit. When we arrived we sought out the 'dug out'. It still looked rather new. But reedbeds have been set and were beginning to spread, islands created from spoil already sprouted a healthy flora, and freshly planted trees and shrubs were doing well.

At the start of the previous winter, whooper swans – flying south from Siberia – found, as had been hoped, the new stretch of water. It met with their approval, they landed, and stayed until the spring. A most encouraging start.

We went into the hide which overlooked the lake. Four great crested grebes, six mallards and five tufted ducks were feeding on the aquatic creatures which had already colonised the water.

Two cuckoos flew down to settle on the wire fence. Five reed buntings preened at the pool's edge. A charm of eight goldfinches hovered and pecked at parachuting thistle seeds and a yellowhammer perched close, wheezing its summer song.

We left the hide and went to explore the rest of the Power Station grounds. An area of old meadows, spinneys, ancient hedgerows and a hidden-away pond forms the Reedholme Reserve which is also managed by the Yorkshire Wildlife Trust.

British Trust for Conservation Volunteers were at work in Reedholme, constructing a nature trail funded with money from the Queen's Silver Jubilee Appeal Trust. It was to be a nature trail with a difference, designed with the visually handicapped in mind. There were to be listening posts with recorded messages, sturdy steps set into inclines, handrails at strategic points and gates adapted for guide dogs.

I walked partway along the trail, closing my eyes from time to time, imagining myself blind, unable to see. I concentrated on smell and sound and taste. It was a good cowslip year. The creamy yellow flowers grew in profusion on the slopes of an old railway embankment. On my hands and knees and with my eyes shut, I could smell their faint scent.

Hawthorn and oak had colonised the same embankment. I picked a hawthorn leaf. Young and tender, it tasted nutty, the 'bread and cheese' of country children. All the time I was attempting to identify by ear bird noises in the spinney: a jay screeched raucously; 'My toe hurts Betty,' crooned a woodpigeon; a tiny wren ticked its loud emphatic alarm notes; and over and over a willow warbler trilled.

The frenzied excavations of a wooing mole gripped by spring fever were evident and, acting blind, I could feel how close together were positioned his little hills of excavated earth.

My fingers explored the rough crinkly texture of lichen, the fragile feel of flower petals, the coolness of young leaves and the soft springy sponginess of mosses.

I stopped being blind as my feet squelched over marshy ground where common spotted orchids grew to pick my way across medieval ridge-and-furrow pasture. Black and white cows grazed so picturesquely that one expected at any moment an eighteenth-century milkmaid to come prancing out from behind a white-blossomed bush with her three-legged wooden milking stool.

On our way back we called in at the field centre, a converted ex-shunter's cabin. Mounted bird wings, stuffed mammals, galls, acorns, nests, seed heads, fungi, grasses – all sorts of natural objects were on view, or 'on feel', for folk who can't see, but for whom tactile experience of different shapes and textures is a small compensation. Schoolchildren had created a three-dimensional map of the reserve with sensitive fingertips in mind.

Pre-recorded cassettes, designed to be used on the nature trail, can be loaned to groups, or bought at cost price. Right from the start of the project, the advice of local visually handicapped people has been sought; it is their suggestions which have been taken up and used at Reedholme.

It was time to go. We made our way to the car park. Walking past trees and hedgerows we heard more birdsong, blackbird, song thrush, robin. And, backing this melodic chorus, we were aware of another noise – as we had been on and off throughout the day – the all-pervasive hum of the power station transformers.

Notable for Nightingales
Monks Wood, Cambridgeshire

Monks Wood, the last remaining fragment of the great Ewingswode Forest, is owned and managed by the Nature Conservancy Council. On request, the East Midlands Region Office of the NCC supplied us with permits to visit.

It was a damp Sunday. The preceding week had seen days of heavy downpour and we came prepared for floods. We parked the cars beside the Institute of Terrestrial Ecology's Experimental Station (Monks Wood is the most thoroughly researched wood in the country!) and changed into our wellingtons.

The song of a nightingale greeted us at the entrance to Hotel Glade. To hear a nightingale sing was the main purpose of our visit. Monks Wood is notable for its nightingales. To experience singing quite so soon was the nicest sort of welcome.

'We're loused out with nightingales this year,' said the Warden, unromantically.

All morning, as we negotiated puddles in the wet clay soil, we were to hear the lovely sound. Nightingales return to Monks Wood in mid-April each year and they sing, both by night and by day, until early June. Always the song of the nightingale sends shivers down my spine – because of its amazing variety, its richness and power and sheer quality.

More birdsong: willow warbler, wren, robin – all in the first few minutes. We walked down the woodland ride, past clumps of early purple orchids, past a wild service tree, and past ditches in which grew the tall pendulous sedge, its attractive female flowers swaying in the breeze. A furry white ermine moth clung to one of the spikes. Above, the purring song of a turtle dove reverberated.

Another nightingale. Its voice carried, but it sang unseen. Nightingales appreciate an open tree canopy with plenty of dense undergrowth and thicket below to provide nesting sites and shelter. Management policy on the reserve includes a regular coppicing-with-standards rotation, providing the songsters with the habitat they seek.

The practice of coppicing has a long history in Britain. For centuries trees were cut at an early stage to encourage timber to grow from the stumps: ash, field maple, hazel, hornbeam. The resulting straight thin poles were readily saleable. But the practice fell into decline after World War I. When coppicing is reinstated in nature reserves where once they bred, the number of nightingales is likely to increase.

Many of the rides in Monks Wood are wide, measuring up to sixty feet across. Wide rides are colonised by woodland edge flowers. The well-mown central track grades into taller herbs, into scrub and into high woodland. Along the ride edges grow cowslip, cuckoo flower, greater stitchwort, wood spurge, wood violet, bugle, yellow archangel and wild strawberry. Flowers attract butterflies – and Monks Wood is famous for its butterflies.

An orangetip settled on the mauve-white petals of lady's smock (or cuckoo flower). It was a male orangetip with orange tips to the black-edged wings and a black centre spot. It closed its wings momentarily and the delicate moss-green mottling on the undersides showed.

A female soon flitted by. No orange tips, but the same green dappling on underwings. A green-veined white (male) fluttered down, landed briefly, realised its mistake – and flew off.

The two species live as adults for only 12–16 days; in this short time a mate must be found. Eggs are laid and the caterpillar hatches out, to feed avidly on seed pods of hedge garlic, lady's smock, charlock or dame's violet for about 25 days. Then it pupates and hibernates through the winter in the chrysalis state – unusually; most butterfly species hibernate as adults or, occasionally, as caterpillars.

In a shaft of sunlight a pair of speckled wood butterflies pirouetted, velvety brown and cream. Up and down they flitted – one male defending its

'A speckled wood basked in the sun.'

territorial patch against the other – spiralling round and round, butterfly bickering. The interloper gave in and flew off in dizzy flight, back down the ride. The victor settled in the long grass, wings outspread to show the four pairs of conspicuous circle 'eyes', scenting the air to attract a female, and to warn off males.

We followed a winding path past hawthorn, dogwood, spindle, guelder-rose, willow, wayfaring tree and dense thickets of blackthorn. In a scalloped sun-trap glade carpeted with misty bluebells a blackcap sang.

The yaffle call of the green woodpecker rang out and, in the distance, came the drumming sound of a lesser spotted woodpecker. Woodpeckers take advantage of the old trees which are left purposely to rot to provide good holes for tree-nesting birds – for rotten wood harbours a bountiful supply of beetles. Good management again!

Woodwalton Fen

From Monks Wood, we drove on to Woodwalton Fen, another National Nature Reserve, again managed by the Nature Conservancy Council. Access is restricted to permit holders and we had booked in advance.

The warden looked worried. 'I considered putting off your visit,' he said, 'the fen is awash after all that rain.'

It turned out that much of Woodwalton would be inaccessible to us that day. We promised to stick to the 'drier' route which he outlined to us.

A snipe was drumming as, obeying instructions and on the lookout for floods, we walked the long bank of a high dyke wall. Circling round, it climbed steeply, then dived with beating wings and fanned tail. The 'thrumming' noise is made by the vibrating of the two separated outermost tail feathers: 'huhuhuhuhuhu'. A snipe's drumming is one of the nicest of early year sounds.

Woodwalton Fen is a surviving fragment of reedswamp and open water, of woodland carr and wet heath which, at one time, covered a vast area of Cambridgeshire and Lincolnshire. From the seventeenth century onwards, much of this land to the south of the Wash was drained and it has been farmed · intensively ever since. Woodwalton stands an oasis, surrounded by sunken arable land.

In 1910, the Hon Charles Rothschild purchased 138 hectares of this fenland fragment and declared it a nature reserve. In the years to follow he purchased a further 70 hectares and asked the Society for the Promotion of Nature Reserves – now the renamed Royal Society for Nature Conservation – to take it into safe keeping.

To preserve Woodwalton as a wetland has been a constant challenge for the Nature Conservancy Council, which leased Woodwalton Fen from the RSNC in 1954. The NCC is determined to maintain its distinctive scenery and very special flora and fauna for such wetlands, sadly, are always under threat.

We walked along the intersecting dyke walls and met a voluntary warden eager to talk to us about some of the work carried out on the reserve. Dykes and channels must be kept clear to ensure a constant flow of water. Invading

'Water violets filled the dyke.'

scrub is removed with heavy machinery and burnt. Former open areas of reed and mixed fen vegetation are being steadily reclaimed. Clay-cored banks have been constructed to form a waterproof perimeter which successfully isolates the reserve. A sluice system, enabling water to be taken in from external drains and retained, has finally resolved the constant threat of 'drying out'.

Down dived a switchback snipe once more, 'huhuhuhuhu'. Striped plumage, dark head stripes, shining white undercarriage and ludicrously long beak.

Now we could hear nightingales again, singing against each other in the woodland scrub. Ankle deep in mud, we squelched across a meadow, stopping to admire the spread of water-violet

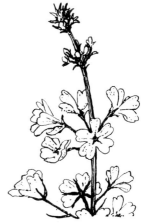

'Pale lilac flowers of water-violet.'

which filled a dyke, whorls of pale lilac flowers encircling straight stems. Other wetland flowers would open later in the year; the tall marsh sowthistle which bears yellow flowers, purple and yellow loosestrife, marsh orchid, water crowfoot, hemp agrimony, meadowrue, and great banks of comfrey.

On an area of heath to the south, we found the scented bog myrtle and, on a newly constructed bank, grew the very rare fen violet. Fen violet seed can lie dormant for long periods until conditions are right; disturbed peat caused by scrub clearance – or the trampling of cattle. It is the excavating of earth for bank construction at Woodwalton that has resulted in the re-emergence of the tiny fen violet flowers.

In such a habitat is also found the great water dock, food plant of the reserve's most notable butterfly, the large copper. Woodwalton's 'speciality', it became extinct in the nineteenth century, but was reintroduced from Holland in 1927 and can be seen on the wing in July.

We were watching a tree pipit in display flight when a sudden downpour took us by surprise and sent us scurrying, as fast as the boggy ground would allow, to the nearest hide. It looked on to a pool, one of several small pools created by the removal of clay for the reserve's perimeter wall. Rain sheeted down on gadwall, tufted duck, coot and mallard.

A cuckoo flew low over the reedbed, to be mobbed at once by two reed warblers. She would probably wait patiently to seize her chance at egg laying, then steal in, for reed warblers are primary hosts to cuckoos in wetland habitat. The warblers' own young are turfed out of the deeply cupped reed nest by the cuckoo chick soon after it hatches and the foster parents find themselves feeding an enormous monster with a huge red gape and insatiable appetite – a monster which will eventually grow to three times their size.

Rain forced us to curtail our visit. A moorhen's nest floating away on a swollen dyke told a sad story.

But our last memory was of a nightingale pair, singing in competition in territories perhaps too close for comfort. As we approached they flew out, sparred for a brief moment, and then returned to songposts across the dyke-divide. The lovely song had haunted us, but this was our only satisfactory nightingale *sighting* of the day.

For such a brief spell each year the bird is with us, its range in Britain restricted to lowlands south-east of a line from the Wash to the Severn estuary. The breeding season is short, eleven weeks; the incubation period is thirteen days and the young fledge in less than two weeks. Single-brooded, some nightingales start the flight south – to tropical savannah, or thorny scrub – at the end of July. Others follow in August. So to catch the song – those wonderful liquid notes and trills and 'jug-jug-jugs' – before the few brief weeks are over, is an experience that never fails to thrill.

Fledgling cuckoo

J · U · N · E

Birds of the Heath

Suffolk Sandlings

We must have looked an odd bunch to any passing motorist catching us in his headlights.

Dense clouds of midges had forced us to turn up collars and to tuck trousers into socks. As we crossed over the road we slapped fiercely with bracken fronds at the itchy swarms. The night was sultry hot and there was thunder in the air.

We were on heathland beyond Minsmere, a relict of the Suffolk Sandlings. So many people rush to Minsmere Reserve, the deservedly popular showpiece owned and managed by the Royal Society for the Protection of Birds; they tot up the number of species seen on the delectable lagoons and marshes – and forget other habitats in the county which also shelter rather special birds.

So we had spent the day enjoying all that magic Minsmere has to offer – avocets and chicks, black-tailed godwits, marsh harriers soaring overhead, a heavy-flying purple heron, little terns . . . And tonight we were defying the midges on a remaining fragment of the once extensive heathland.

It was an hour after sunset and already dark enough to pick out glow-worms in the bracken sparking brightly with a greenish light. Over the sandy soil we walked, past Scots pines black against the night sky, past silver birch, gorse and heather and all the while we listened intently for night sounds.

Suddenly a high-pitched 'tsiwick' rang out. In slow-flapping flight a bird

flew over the tree tops. Again the abrupt call, followed by growling croaks: 'kwark, kwark'. It dropped back down into cover, a roding woodcock.

The woodcock is an anomaly: a woodland wader. In many ways, it is more like an owl than a wader, with its rounded wings, nocturnal habits, and adaptations to a woodland way of life. But its long bill, silhouetted against the darkening sky as it flew over, is wader-like – and so is its cryptic plumage.

These strange elusive birds indulge in extravagant display flights during the breeding season. The roding male circles his territory at treetop level, patrolling boundaries with deliberation at dusk and giving the ritual eerie call.

It was a good start to our evening. The wind was blowing cooler now. The moon, at its full, was swathed in mist. Out of the stillness, a lone nightingale began to sing. We stood and listened. Pure, clear, far-carrying. Night time is the best time to hear the nightingale – when it sings alone.

Following a path eastwards through the heather, we came to the edge of the heathland, where silver birches had invaded the bracken. And another sound: the strangely vibrating, deep churring, of a nightjar.

A long-tailed, hawk-like bird emerged from the trees, dusky shape in the gloom. It wheeled silently over our heads, circled again, clapped its wings, and dropped back down into silver birches to resume its mechanical sonorous crooning, 'Krrrrrrrrrrr-oo, krrrrrrrrrrr-oo'. Weird, it sounded. We stood there in the dark, imagining the bird crouched on a branch, turning its head from side to side, slurring from pitch to pitch.

A second nightjar started up at a few yards distant. Territories were close. Both birds churred their rattle notes warningly at each other, their mates (most likely) on ground-nests below. Shadowy shapes changed position, flying noiselessly, giving brief glimpses.

It was getting very late. The moon shone brightly now. The earlier mist had dispersed. A small mammal – vole? mouse? – scurried across our path. As we walked back down the track, the nightingale was still singing.

Breckland, Norfolk

The next day we went to Breckland to look for a bird that some people think of as 'a bit of a bustard'. The last *great* bustard disappeared from Britain early in the nineteenth century. By 1840 not a single individual remained. Unfortunately for a bustard, its flesh tastes good. 'Like Welsh mutton', according to one report. Gourmets lured them to piles of turnips, then shot at them with duck-guns.

We shall probably never again be able to witness in the Breck the spectacular 'balloon' display of the great bustard. Two hundred years ago, early morning watchers in the sand dunes could have been rewarded by the sight of male bustards inflating their throat pouches into balloons, and extravagantly flaunting their plumages to a bizarre extent in their efforts to

Heron

attract a female; white undertail feathers and white underwings were raised high, forced forward, almost turned inside out – and fanned invitingly.

However, today we were seeking, not the long-gone bustard, but the nearest Breckland can offer to such a strange bird: the stone curlew.

The stone curlew was at one time classified in close proximity to the Otididae on the Systematic List of British Birds and declared to be an Otididae-oddity: a close relation of the bustard. But later experts looked again at the 'knees' (actually its 'ankle' tarsal joints) and at other parts of its anatomy. In spite of its bustard-like habits and looks, they decided it must be a wader, a Norfolk plover, and a member of the Burhinidae family. ('Burhinidae' means 'thick knees'.)

'That strange bird, the stone curlew.'

We left the car and, armed with NNT permits, headed for a hide belonging to the Norfolk Naturalists' Trust. A sudden hubbub stopped us in our tracks. Wheatears clicked furiously. Lapwings swooped and pee-witted madly. Two red-legged partridges scurried by in a panic. All was agitation. A *stoat* had invaded the territory.

It sat up like a squirrel, its spruce brown back tinted chestnut in the sunlight, its belly cream-coloured. Then it ran, dodging between sandy hillocks, black-tipped tail undulating behind as it attempted to escape the constant buzzing of irate birds.

It ran – stopped – ran. Almost as if it were playing a game. Frantic parents continued to hassle and swear and at last the stoat grew tired and bounded off into the cover of a pine tree windbreak. The fuss and commotion died down.

A wheatear, in celebration perhaps, flew up and then descended in a slow 'butterfly' display flight. Lapwing chicks emerged from hiding, the fluffiest of tiny balls, speckled, with white collars and white fronts. And all this time the rabbits had nibbled on, unperturbed – in spite of the fact that rabbits often provide the stoat with a third of its daily food requirements.

We continued to the hide and, through the slits, peered out on to a wilderness of sandy hills and hollows, sparse grass, scattered hawthorn bushes and wind-bent pines. Like the great bustard, stone curlews are happiest in a semi-desert habitat and Breckland, on the Norfolk/Suffolk border, supplies the nearest we have in Britain to such steppe-like conditions.

Summers in Breck are hot and dry; winters, cold and bleak. Rainfall is light. Vegetation is very special, continental in character. Here the Spanish catchfly and the rare spiked speedwell can be found.

'Curr-*ee*, curr-*ee* . . .'. A thin eerie whistling. 'The whistle of the Norfolk plover,' wrote W. G. Clarke in his book *In Breckland Wilds* (1925) 'is typical of the freedom of the wild, the heart of solitude, spaces where the wind wanders sobbing and wailing.'

A sizeable bird (about as large as an oystercatcher) appeared on a low, rounded dune, silhouetted against the skyline. It stood, hunched and short-necked. I focussed my binoculars on the prominent amber-yellow eyes. And the long legs with the knobbly tarsal 'knees'. It stepped slowly and with deliberation, head jutting forward, then paused, its streaky plumage a cryptic sandy-brown: the colour of its sandy background.

We began to notice more individuals and counted six birds, although there may have been others in the hollows. We listened for whistles, and sorted out pairs. Stone curlews winter in southern Europe. They return to the Breck from the Mediterranean in mid-March and early April. Two blotchy eggs are laid in a shallow scrape and incubated by both parents in turn.

Already young had hatched – even more difficult to spot. But two tiny heads bobbed up and two downy chicks came into view, teetered over the sand then flopped out of sight again: balls of speckled cinnamon fluff.

Rabbits bunny-hopped from burrows. Their role in stone curlew ecology, and the ecology of other Breckland birds, is vital. They close-crop the turf thus helping to preserve the very specialised habitat.

A stone curlew on the ground may be inconspicuous but, in flight, it is striking. A bird skimmed low over the dunes, its long wings, unfolded, revealed a pattern of black and white. It landed, ran a few steps, closed its wings and slowed to a halt.

But mostly our birds just skulked, inactive. It is at night that they come to life, stalking prey between dusk and dawn, peering with those large yellow eyes. A sudden dart, a quick jab with the stout bill – and beetle, moth, woodlouse or spider gets snapped up abruptly.

We left the hide with regret, but there was more of Breckland to explore. 'Breck' means 'land that has been broken up'.

For centuries farmers have intermittently striven to break up and tame for cultivation the miles of wide treeless deserts. Bone-dry, heather-covered and undulating with sandswept low dunes, Breck and its enormous population of rabbits defeated the farmers time and time again. Some turned to sheep grazing, and 'warreners' exploited the rabbits commercially.

But in the twentieth century the farmers and foresters have tamed the Breck at last. Heavy machinery has irrevocably changed the landscape and much of it is now under the plough – or planted with coniferous trees. Inevitably stone curlew numbers have dropped. Fewer than 200 pairs remain in the whole of East Anglia.

But the bird is adapting. It now nests beside the busy runways of the American fighter-bomber base at RAF Lakenheath, and resignedly lays its eggs amongst the corn, beet, pea and carrot crops growing in its traditional haunts. Nests are found, too, in the wide rides of the new forests, and in young plantations where trees are not too tall.

The Suffolk and Norfolk Trusts are anxious to protect the remaining precious heathland, of such particular interest to naturalists; they already own a number of reserves and want to acquire more.

We wandered on, enjoying the flowers which grew on the arid soil: black meddick, heath bedstraw, spring vetch, storksbill, red fescue, wild pansy, scarlet pimpernel. Tufts of sand sedge, precisely spaced, pushed through the sandy soil from nodules on long underground roots.

Butterflies abounded: we saw small copper, green hairstreak, grizzled skipper, orangetip, painted lady, common blue, speckled wood, small heath, wall brown and red admiral.

Now we were in forest. Three bright redstarts darted in and out of piles of brushwood in a clearing. A woodlark rose, spiralling from a fir. It hung, fluttering its wings, hovering – and then wavered gently downwards, back into the trees.

'Short tail,' pronounced an expert, 'diagnostic feature of the woodlark.' We could not hear its lovely song for a vociferous skylark (with *long* tail) was trilling directly overhead.

The day grew hotter. Ominous thunder rolls threatened rain. Now the clouds burst. A short downpour drenched us, but it lasted only a few minutes. The sun shone once more and our clothes steamed dry.

We were nearing a traditional red-backed shrike patch. Gorse was ablaze with yellow blossom. We looked for thorn-impaled insects, victims of the 'butcher-bird', but found none.

No shrike. But stoat, butterflies, woodlark, redstart, wheatear, lapwing – and stone curlews – to remind us of the days when the great bustard roamed the wild sandy spaces of Breck in droves.

Eagles of Arran

Isle of Arran, Scotland

The Isle of Arran is easy to reach from the mainland in summer. The car ferry runs several times a day. Arran is the most southerly of the Inner Hebridean islands, 15 miles away from Ardrossan on the Ayrshire coast. It is 10 miles across and 19 miles from north to south. The coastal perimeter road is 56 miles long.

It is a splendid island with prolific bird life, abundant flowers, red deer silhouettes on the skyline, white crofts, stone circles, fine natural harbours and jagged mountain peaks.

On the shingle beach, where the burnet rose grows, ringed plovers incubate eggs in shallow scrapes. Just offshore, red-breasted mergansers dive smoothly after fish. Oystercatchers pipe relentlessly in showy flypasts. In an early-summer creche, small stripy shelducks are shepherded about the bay by earnest 'aunties'.

The peaty brown moorland rises up into the hills and makes for rough walking. Sheep paths lead through the bracken. Burns tumble and splash. White bog cotton-grass warns of wet patches. Up in the hills are the gull colonies, herring gull and lesser black-backed, on the shores of inland wind-swept lochs. The unwary climber is dive-bombed by irate parent birds as speckled chicks freeze to stillness behind clumps of raffia-like moor grass.

But the main purpose of our trip to Arran was to see the golden eagle. Two pairs hold territory on the island. But where?

We bought a copy of the weekly newspaper, *The Arran Banner*. We read of rescue by helicopter of the Pladda Lighthouse Keeper, of an around-Arran sponsored walk, of the twenty-three goals scored against Southend United by the Lamlash football team. Then, on page 7, we read, 'John Rhead. Hill birds all day trail. Meet Lochranza Golf Car Park. Great views of Golden Eagle on last week's trail.'

So at 10.30 the next morning we found ourselves waiting at Lochranza, the most northerly point of the island. 'Fair Loch Ranza, the lone hamlet which her inland bay/And circling mountains sever from the world,' wrote Sir Walter Scott.

John Rhead arrived and, after only a few minutes, we knew we had found a genuine birder. A local man with eyes like a hawk's, a sound knowledge of the terrain and a fund of good 'birdy' stories, he inspired us with optimism. If John Rhead couldn't find golden eagles for us, then no-one could.

He led us up a steep track until we were 1,000 feet above the long Lochranza inlet. Grey seals basked on boulders in a flat calm in Scott's 'inland bay', close to the ruins of the historic castle. Stands of yellow iris blossomed on the black tidal silt of the shoreline. Far out, white shoots of spray marked where gannets from Ailsa Craig plummetted into the sea after fish.

We could see more islands, Bute, Jura, Great Cumbrae, Islay. Then we turned our backs and walked into the hills. Rabbits scurried at our approach. Small moorland birds 'clink'-ed their alarm. Wheatears, whinchats, stonechats – all share call notes akin to the clinking sound of pebbles, had we noticed? said John.

He pointed out a family group of 'hoodies'. Hooded crows are a northern form of the carrion crow. Where hoodies and carrions meet – as they do on Arran – hybridisation occurs. But, high in the hills, true hoodies are common with pale grey bodies, black heads, black tails and black wings. Beneath a stunted rowan tree the group was busily engaged, perhaps feasting on a rabbit carcase.

A glossy black raven flew by: 'Diamond-shaped tail,' said John. Meadow pipits rose, singing, into the air, and 'tseep-tseep'-ed down again in a slow parachute descent.

Suddenly our guide stopped. 'There!' he exclaimed triumphantly. We followed his pointing finger. A flock of gulls . . . and a great soaring bird with long broad wings. Golden eagle! It rose upwards and away from the harassing gulls, tilted, and swept strongly and fast across the sky. Heavy head, long tail,

'The eagle swept across the sky.'

rectangular wings. It disappeared from sight behind the slope of the hill. Then reappeared, gliding, soaring. And a *second* eagle followed.

John told us that he had devoted many hours the previous year in observation of the golden eagles of Arran, recording their every move. First he had had to apply for permission (not easy to get) from the Nature Conservancy Council. The golden eagle, at one time persecuted to near extinction by gamekeepers, is now a strictly protected bird.

Eagles start to breed in their fifth year. They are a long-lived species and a pair will not lay eggs every year. Mostly just one chick survives. The first to hatch often kills its younger siblings soon after they emerge from the eggs: the 'Cain and Abel syndrome'.

The eagles vanished from sight and we walked on. 'Watch out for adders basking in the sun,' warned John, 'this track is known as "adders' path".'

The bubbling notes of a female cuckoo rang out as, rounding a bend and finding ourselves with the sea again in view, we settled to picnic. Above us, on a ledge, the conspicuous white breast feathers of a male peregrine caught John's eye. He pointed it out to us. It was not the falcon's nesting site; John wisely keeps all such eyries a closely guarded secret; Scotland has more than its fair share of egg stealers.

The bird took off. With a burst of terrific speed it headed out to sea. 'Watch,' said John. 'I think we might be going to see a kill – perhaps a pigeon. Keep your binocs on him.'

Fast and furiously he flew. We kept him in view until he was just a speck in the distance. There, a second speck. It was another peregrine: his mate? We were not to see the famous 'stoop' dive on to prey after all. The two falcons flew together and disappeared into cloud.

That wasn't the last of the day's raptors. As we began our slithery descent to the shore, a kestrel hovered above the brow of the hill. Below us, the pale grey shape of a quartering male hen harrier flew back and forth over reedbeds, until it spied prey – and on an instant dropped to the ground.

We weren't far away from the ruins of an old settlement, abandoned at the time of the dreadful Clearances by islanders who, driven by impossible conditions, bravely set out for the unknown territories of Canada to start their lives afresh.

We were walking downhill now and reached the shingle to head north for the Cock of Arran. A buzzard hung in the wind, balancing on a current of air. Over-eager birdwatchers are tempted to 'turn' buzzards into eagles. Size is often difficult to judge, but the rounded wings of the buzzard are so much shorter that once the sheer length of an eagle's wings has been experienced, it is impossible to mistake the two.

We scrambled over a great fall of rocks, and jumped over burns trickling into the sea. Across the water the Mull of Kintyre was shrouded in mist but on the Cock of Arran the sun still shone. Beneath the cliff nestled primroses, ragged robin, pink thrift, sea campion, birdsfoot trefoil, yellow pimpernel, milkwort.

Two sandpipers landed lightly on a boulder and raised their wings high in a courtship gesture. The cooing calls of eider ducks carried across the bay, 'Ooooooo-OO-oo, oooooooo-OO-oo.'

We continued full circle back to Lochranza. Two more golden eagle sightings were ours on the way. We had the expertise of our guide to thank. John knew exactly where to bring us. His long experience of birdwatching in the hills of Arran had taught him the best vantage points.

But no bird can ever be *guaranteed. Luck*, too, was with us that day.

Dean Watch

Forest of Dean, Gloucestershire

'So what do you want to see?' asked the Warden of Nagshead RSPB Reserve.

'Redstarts, pied flycatchers, woodpeckers, wood warblers, nuthatches . . .'

'Then you must make yourselves invisible,' he said. 'Follow the waymarked paths, keep your distance from birds feeding their young – and skulk.'

The Forest of Dean, set between two rivers, the Wye and the Severn, is one of Britain's few remaining ancient forests. The Forestry Commission owns the bulk of its 28,500 acres and manages several nature reserves jointly with bodies such as the Nature Conservancy Council, Royal Society for the Protection of Birds and the Gloucestershire Trust for Nature Conservation.

Waymarked paths, planned with the help of the Ramblers' Association, are helpful innovations; coloured arrows painted on posts at junctions mark the trails.

On this day in early June, the foliage was so lush, and the birds at this crucial young-rearing stage so wary that, although we could *hear* birds all around us, not a glimpse of a feather would we see – unless we followed the Warden's advice, and skulked.

I crept off down a little path through curling bracken. Pink foxgloves grew tall. Bluebells were fading has-beens but yellow pimpernel, white stitchwort and the tiny flowers of blue milkwort brightened the grass of a small clearing.

With my back against the stout trunk of an oak tree I crouched still, hoping that my green anorak was blending nicely with the surround, and trying to ignore the gnats which promptly and itchily invaded my scalp.

Our locale was one of the best remaining stands of oak in the Forest. In the sixteenth century the Spanish Armada, before its abortive attempt to invade Britain, was ordered to destroy, if nothing else, the oak trees of the

Forest of Dean above the River Wye

Nuthatch

Forest of Dean. From the oak came the timber with which British ships were built.

Oak woodland is well known to be particularly rich in many species of bugs, thrips, aphids, beetles, gall wasps, leaf miners and moth caterpillars, all chomping away at leaves, twigs, buds – or each other. An oak tree, to a bird, must equal a fresh-food, self-service, take-away delicatessen.

The critical breeding season coincides with peak insect population. Hatching of eggs synchronises with the annual 'bloom' of caterpillars. Foliage-gleaning birds pick insects off the leaves; bark-investigators probe with sharp beaks into cracks; ground-feeders scavenge for caterpillars which have dropped from trees in order to pupate.

A wren scrabbled in leaf litter a few yards away: tiny, rufous-brown, pert-tailed. Then it hopped into bramble cover and was lost from view. It 'tick'ed vigorously and, a moment later, burst into dramatic song.

Singing from several other species, hidden completely by the dense canopy of leaves, tantalised. Robins, willow warblers, blackbirds, song thrushes, blue tits, great tits teased with their nearness – and invisibility.

Forty feet away was a nestbox fixed to a tree trunk at a height of 8 feet above the ground. I waited patiently, sitting very still, for the arrival of its occupant. A delightful small black and white bird appeared: a male pied flycatcher. He flew to a dead branch, paused for a moment, and then darted in through the hole of the nestbox. A moment later he emerged. Through my binoculars I could see the white wing bars and the slightly bizarre face pattern: two small blobs of white – like false eyes – on his forehead.

Pied flycatchers have been the subject of study in the Forest of Dean ever since 1942 when the first eighty boxes were nailed into place. More boxes are added each year and checked periodically.

Pied-fly's arrive at the end of April from tropical Africa and are on the move again in July; the short breeding season lasts about forty days. Sociable little birds, they take readily to boxes in lieu of holes in trees. 'The more boxes, the more pied flycatchers,' conclude naturalists. Pied-fly numbers have increased dramatically since nestbox provision has become widespread practice in the sessile oakwoods they prefer.

A brown and white female appeared with a cranefly in her beak. She landed on a twig, took stock, and shot into the box – to feed her brood.

I crept back the few yards to the waymarked path and walked on down the track. Sessile oaks? I inspected an over-hanging branch. The leaves had distinct short stalks, a clue that it was a sessile oak. But the acorns, when they appeared, would be *un*stalked ('sessile'=sitting). Leaves of pedunculate oaks are generally unstalked; the acorns grow on stalks (peduncles). But hybridisation between pedunculate and sessile oaks, the two oak species native to Britain, often occurs in areas where both are found. Sessile oakwoods are commonest on the poorer acid soils of the north and west and the characteristic openness and lack of shrub layer beneath the canopy proves attractive to a certain bird clientele, including the pied flycatchers.

'T-t-t-trrrrrrrrr peu, peu, peu'. Wood warbler song. A single note lead-up to a shivering trill, followed by clear, far-carrying, falling whistles. I climbed up on to a bank to see. On the lower branch of a hazel tree, a greenish bird with a very white belly was singing vigorously. Its sulphur-yellow throat was visibly pulsating with the effort. Wood warblers are another typical bird of sessile oakwoods.

A caterpillar dangled in front of me, hanging in mid-air by a silver thread attached to an oak tree twig. It was so close that I could see the tiny ball of silk held between its front pair of legs and its jaws. It jerked and looped and lurched energetically, finally landing upon an oak leaf. It then snapped the thread, and the minute silver ball swung gently free. Scrunch, scrunch; it began to eat the leaf.

I wandered on a little further, catching glimpses through the trees of a deep valley and hills beyond. I met other birdwatchers and we swopped sightings. I was told to look out for a redstart at the next bend, its black face and chestnut tail showing for brief moments as it darted into the open, out and back, fly-catching.

An adder had been seen; it slowly wound its way along the track before sensing intruders and slithering off into cover. Obligingly it had allowed time for everyone to note its zig-zag back stripe ending with the V on its head.

Someone else had watched, in icky fascination, two large slugs in the process of a slimy mating; a complicated business, for each slug is both male and female, and both ooze away to lay eggs!

'Listen for the hawfinch, "ptik" . . . and a garden warbler singing high in a beech tree where an opening in the trees overlooks the valley.' And a cinnamon and blue nuthatch had been seen creeping up the trunk of a tree towards its mud-patched nesting hole, giving one lad a splendid chance to try out his new birthday present telescope.

All the same, 'tantalising' was the word I heard most often from birdwatchers that day. A cuckoo flew over, calling loudly, invisible above the canopy of leaves. Just a glimpse did I get of a boldly patterned – red, black and white – great spotted woodpecker, and yet its drumming was constantly in my ears.

A jay appeared – momentary flash of azure blue wings – to screech and vanish. Jackdaws flocked noisily at the back of the wood; only occasionally did their silhouettes show black against the sky.

We kept our distance from nests and stuck close to paths, very conscious of the vulnerability of young birds and the urgent searchings for food of anxious parents. By the end of the day each of us had our own small nest-egg of vivid memories to take home and treasure. The Forest of Dean in June is both tantalising – and very rewarding.

Scenic Trail

Lake Vyrnwy, Powys

The scenic Lake Vyrnwy Nature Trail begins at the ornate Victorian dam and leads up through woodland, both deciduous and coniferous, into the heathery hills.

In the 1880s, the expanding population of Liverpool led to an increased demand for water. It was decided to flood the glacial valley of Vyrnwy at the south-western end of the Berwyn Mountains. With its steep sides, flat impermeable rock floor and narrow bottle-neck shape, it was an ideal site for a reservoir. Villagers were moved to higher ground, the great barrage was built, and the flooding began.

Today a narrow road follows closely the eleven mile perimeter of inlets and bays. Trees, planted in generous numbers, have grown and spread from the shoreline upwards into the hills. There is little to show, apart from the dam, that the lake is man-made and not natural.

The Royal Society for the Protection of Birds obtained a twenty-one-year agreement with the Severn–Trent Water Authority which allows them to manage best for wildlife the 16,000 acres of the Vyrnwy Estate.

We parked in the car park and picked up copies of the RSPB-designed trail leaflet at the Visitor Centre, a converted stone chapel. This chapel was built after the flooding, to serve the new village. Now it is no longer used for worship, but acts as a useful starting point to the day's walking. Should we do the short route? or the long? The long, of course!

We turned our backs on the reservoir and walked through sessile oak and birch woodland to 'Stop One'. Already we could hear the 'tea-cher, tea-cher' call of the great tit and the 'pink-pink'ing of chaffinches. Many of the nestboxes nailed to trunks of trees were occupied. Of those positioned each year well over half are used, by blue tits, great tits, marsh tits, pied flycatchers, nuthatches, redstarts and tawny owls.

Detouring a little, we crossed over the alder-fringed river by footbridge. A great spotted woodpecker was climbing, with little jerky-jump movements, its tail braced, up the trunk of a dead conifer. Disdaining man-made boxes, it had excavated its own hole – into which it now disappeared.

Thirty yards on, a 'little brown job' sat very upright on a wire fence. Then out – and back – it shuttled. And again. Typical behaviour of the spotted flycatcher – the sally forth, momentary hover, snatch at a fly and return.

We started to climb, accompanied by intermittent snatches of birdsong: wood warbler, garden warbler and willow warbler. But song is less evident in late June. The courtship, territory-defending days have given way to busy days of food-seeking and brood-raising.

We left the trees behind and emerged into the open. House martins and swallows skimmed low after flying insects; more pressurised parents with hungry youngsters to feed.

The sun shone down on the grassy slopes, accentuating petal colour: blue of germander speedwell, pink of campion, mauve of tufted vetch and white of stitchwort. Pignut, a delicate umbellifer, was in flower; and yellow rattle and tormentil.

We were high on the hillslope now. We turned to look back. Below lay the reservoir, offset by the panorama of mountains. A buzzard sailed over the high crags and bare peat moors of Craig y Gribin. It was a picture postcard view and we settled on the grass to enjoy it – and to eat our sandwiches.

Family parties of long-tailed tits trilled and acrobated in the willow scrub close by. We counted the small, pink blobs with their ludicrously long tails. Eleven. The young ones were less strongly coloured and still had a downy look about them.

Then on we walked, over heather moorland now. A wheatear 'chack'ed. 'Weep, chack, chack' it called: erect stance, black eyepatch, corn-coloured breast, grey and black mantle. It flicked its black tail with the heart-shaped white pattern. (The name, 'wheatear', is derived from its earlier name, 'white-arse'!) Wheatears are birds of hilly country, of short turf and boulders, of bracken, and of rabbit holes in which they can nest.

A yellowhammer sang from its perch in a patch of gorse and a grey wagtail flew over. Meadow pipits flitted across the grass and skylarks chirruped. Over 120 species of birds have been recorded on the reserve.

'A wheatear "chack"ed.'

Once more the scenery changed as we entered a plantation of larch, spruce and Douglas fir. A thin squeaking betrayed the presence of two baby goldcrests, precariously balanced on the branch of a larch. A parent bird was feeding them on . . . daddy-long-legs? With much wobbling, the tiny fledglings stretched their wings, fluffed their feathers and hopped in pretend flight.

'Cher-tee, *cher*-tee, *cher*-tee': there was a coal tit, too, in amongst the needles.

Circular clumps of elegant male fern grew from a stone bank beside the track. Foxgloves had opened their mitten flowers. We looked for squirrels – red squirrel and grey squirrel live happily side by side at Vyrnwy – but today they were deep in the forest.

Out into the sunshine again. 'Peacock butterfly,' said Jane. It was sunning itself on the path. Tatty and faded now, it had survived hibernation through the winter. In a few weeks' time this year's peacocks, immaculately spruce, would emerge from pupae.

Next, a steep uphill slog. 'Merits three rests at least,' decided Alan.

Trees up here were young, in a recently planted mixed plantation. Rose-bay willow-herb, not yet in flower, had colonised the cinder track. The finding of a huge wolf spider, tiny sparkling beetles and a glossy, bright-striped bug, gave us excuse to pause and get our breath. Three kestrels diverted with an acrobatic aerial display.

We reached 'Stop Seven', the final halt. We had walked three miles, circling Craig Garth-bwlch. From now on it was downhill all the way, with a marvellous view of Lake Vyrnwy and the possibility of finding goosander, dipper, grey wagtail, sandpiper and kingfisher on its shores and waters to entice us on.

'Wing-Winnowing Lark . . .'

Helpston, Cambridgeshire

We went to Helpston, near Peterborough, to 'see the skylark as he springs/ shake morning moisture from his wings/ and rise and sing to music proud/ as small as a bee beneath the cloud.'

Helpston is the village where John Clare was born in 1793 and the poet knew, from personal experience, at least 145 wild birds. He recorded in prose and verse his observations.

'The wild duck wherries to the distant flood . . .' 'Whizz goes the peewit o'er

the ploughman's team/ with many a whew and whirl and sudden scream . . .'
'A sedge bird built its little benty nest/ close by the meadow-pool and wooden brig . . .'

The cottage next to the Bluebell Inn is Clare's birthplace. 'My early home was paradise,' he wrote in his diary. 'There is nothing but poetry about the existence of childhood.' His parents seemed to have given him every encouragement and his first poems were imitations of his father's songs. He wrote that his mother's 'hopeful ambition ran high of being able to make me a good scholar.'

John was perhaps fortunate in that his was a small family: mother, father, two children. Most villagers were encumbered with the huge broods of the day and it was as much as worn parents could do to keep them warm and fed. But John's parents had time to give. They took an interest in his schooling. John's father, a thresher, was the illegitimate son of a Scottish schoolmaster.

Clare's cottage

With 'triumphant anxiety', they looked on as the boy worked of an evening at his 'sheep-hooks and tarbottles' (handwriting exercises) or struggled with 'a knotty question in Numeration or Pounds shillings and Pence'.

He loved books, bought them when he could, and soon knew much of the writing of past and contemporary poets by heart. His collection, consisting of 440 volumes, can be seen today in Northampton Public Library.

He began to write his own verse whilst still quite young, shyly at first, correcting again and again as his 'second thoughts blushed over his first attempts'. But gradually he gained confidence. Meanwhile he had to keep himself. He worked as labourer, ploughboy, shepherd, gardener, lime-burner and hedge-planter. 'I found the poetry in the fields and only wrote them down,' he explained. 'Birds bees trees and flowers all talk to me incessantly louder than the busy hum of men.'

John would not recognise the Helpston cottage today. Smartened up, it gleams with whitewash under a neat roof of thatch. But sparrows still nest beneath the eaves. Clare had a soft spot for the much-persecuted birds. 'You're welcome here,' he told them, and he wrote, 'Fighting sparrows glad at heart/ chirp in the cottage eaves.'

We left the village and walked across the fields on 'footpath's narrow way' towards Hilly Wood. The sky was full of lark song. Clare wrote many lines in praise of the skylark.

'Wing-winnowing lark with speckled breast . . .' 'The lark with sudden impulse starts and sings/ and mid the smoking rain/ quivers her russet wings . . .' 'Till mixing with the vapour's dun/ he's lost in valleys of the sun . . .' 'Then hangs a dust spot in the sunny skies/ and drops and drops.'

He describes a skylark's nest which he found tucked away in a hoof print: 'Behind a clod/ how snug the nest/ is in a horse's footing fixed/ of twitch and stubbles roughly dressed/ with roots and horsehair intermixed.'

A yellowhammer 'fluttered in short fears' a few yards in front of us. Then flew up and settled on the girder of a pylon, showing off its 'yellow breast and head of solid gold'. In its beak was a large green caterpillar. It must have a nest close by with, perhaps, 'five eggs, pen scribbled o'er with ink/ their shells resembling writing scrolls'.

Black-headed gulls ('cawdy-mawdies') circled the fields as we walked: 'White cawdy-mawdies slow swiver and sail.'

We reached Hilly Wood. Wood pigeons, alarmed, fled with much commotion at our approach. '. . . through many boughs with cluttering noise/ till free from such restraints above their head/ they smacked their clapping wings.' We could hear other birds too. A wren sang exuberantly, with 'short tail ever on the strut/ cocked gadding up above his back.' Chaffinches, which Clare called 'pinks', willow warblers ('pettichaps'), great tits ('blackcaps') and blue tits ('bluecaps'); we heard them all in song, and a blackbird too. 'The

Gannet and young

rich blackbird through his golden bill utters wild music.'

Back down the old Roman road we walked. A cuckoo flew across. 'And cuckoo, quivering upon narrow wing/ take sudden flitting from the neighbouring tree.' Like John Clare we, too, heard its 'full toned anthem with two simple notes'.

A mile's drive south in the car took us to all that remains of Clare's beloved heathland. 'There is a wild and beautiful neglect . . .'

Emmonsailes Heath, now known as Ailsworth Heath, shrank drastically during Clare's life time, the result of the Enclosure Act which was enforced in Helpston in 1809. Clare was sixteen. He raged against the carving up of the land into 'little parcels little minds to please'. He wrote poems in protest, railing against the 'never-weary plough'.

'Enclosure like a Buonaparte let not a thing remain/ it levelled every bush and tree and levelled every hill/ and hung the moles for traitors – though the brook is running still/ it runs a naked stream cold and chill,' he proclaimed vehemently.

The remnant of surviving heathland is owned by the Nature Conservancy Council. Castor Hanglands Reserve is a superb woodland area for birds.

We followed a pleasant bridle path through trees and soon found ourselves listening to the sweet bubbling song of a blackcap. Clare was aware that blackcaps occasionally overwinter, and that their song is sometimes mistaken for that of a nightingale. 'With a rich and such an early song it sings' when 'sallow catkins once all downy white/ turn like the sunshine into golden light . . . yet on the hawthorn scarce a leaf appears.'

A pond had flooded our path in a 'hazel-crowded glen'. We negotiated with care. Three tiny fluffy moorhen chicks, 'a sooty brood', cheeped loudly and paddled for shelter beneath a pile of brushwood. 'Each leaves for water as it leaves the nest,' Clare wrote of moorhen chicks.

A pied wagtail dabbled in the wet. 'The standing pools were covered with a sort of hairy moss/ and the little nodding wagtail/ printed many paths across.'

We emerged from the trees. A hawk flew low, rusty red in the sun's glow, black band visible on its tail; a kestrel. Clare described the kestrel's hover as it hangs 'in the sky on narrow pointed quivering wings', and its plummet to earth: 'The small hawk like a shot drops from the sky/ close to my feet for mice and creeping things.' A climb over a stile – and a redstart sang its short phrases from the branch of an ash: 'The fire-tail's "tweet-tut" fretting call/ keeps up a teasing melody.'

When Clare's first book was published in 1820, he enjoyed a brief fame, including trips to London and contact with other writers. But from then on his life, increasingly, consisted of frustrations and disappointments.

His financial position was often desperate. His wife, Patsy, bore him eight ill-nourished, ailing children. His editors meddled excessively with his work – and then didn't manage to sell it. ('If doctors were as fond of amputations

Dragonflies

as editors are of altering and correcting the world would have nothing but cripples,' he grumbled.) In 1832, he moved away from his beloved Helpston to a larger house in bleak Northborough on the edge of the fens. By 1837 he was an inmate of an asylum in Epping Forest.

Sad though his life was from then on until his death in 1864, his poems – many of them – remained joyful. So often he begins a line with 'I love . . .' 'I love to see . . .' I love to roam . . .' The last poem to survive in manuscript form was a happy one: 'Birds' Nests'.

We drove from Castor Hanglands to Maxey and found the haunted path where Clare had walked 'very fearful' each week as a boy to collect flour from the mill. A low-flying heron did its best to evoke atmosphere; 'The old heron from the lonely lake/ starts slow and flaps his melancholy wings.' And jackdaws in their 'powdered wigs' rose in a flock from fields of maize and sugar beet.

Back in Clare's village house martins skimmed, repairing cup-like nests glued close under the eaves of a farmhouse. 'Round the pond the martins flit/ their snowy breasts bedawbed with dirt/ while the mason 'neath the slates/ each mortar-bearing bird awaits/ untaught by art each labouring spouse/ curious daubs his hanging house.'

Swifts rode high above the roof tops, screeching, swooping after summer gnats. 'Swift goes the sooty swallow . . . swifter than skims the cloud-rack of the skies.'

Peeping over a garden wall, we saw a robin 'watching worms the gardener's spade unbears'. And, under the hedge, a dunnock: 'The tame hedge-sparrow in its russet dress/ is half a robin for its gentle ways.'

Crows acrobated above a dead elm tree, 'The crow will tumble up and down/ at first sign of spring/ and in old trees around the town/ brush winter from its wing.'

On the village green stands a memorial to the poet. Swallows 'twittered gladly by' as we paused to read the lines. We stood by Clare's grave in the churchyard and flocks of starlings flew overhead, 'blackening the evening sky'.

Each year in early July, the John Clare Society holds a festival in Helpston to celebrate the poet's birthday. An excellent Journal, published annually 'to reflect the interest in, and approaches to, the life and work of the poet' will be on sale at the Festival (free to members). It was through the Society's occasional Newsletter that I came to hear about, and attend, a residential weekend course at Horncastle College of Adult Education in Lincolnshire. Rodney Lines, editor of the Newsletter, and Barron Wright taught me much that was new to me about a favourite poet. And, at first opportunity, I went with a fellow Clare admirer to look for John Clare's birds.

The success of the day surprised us both. And we shall see more birds if we visit again in winter when 'The fieldfare chatters in the whistling thorn . . .', 'The wild swan hurries high and noises loud/ with white neck peering to the evening cloud,' and 'Coy bumbarrels [long-tailed tits] twenty in a drove/ Flit down the hedgerows in the frozen plain/ and hang on little twigs and start again.'

James Fisher, the eminent ornithologist, wrote, 'John Clare was the finest poet of British minor naturalists, and the finest naturalist of all Britain's major poets. He fell into some pitfalls . . . but the combination of keen observation with poetic skill, of accuracy with emotion, in his poems is unique in British verse.'

Gannets
Bempton Cliffs, Humberside

A three-mile stretch of the 400-foot high Bempton Cliffs at Flamborough Head is owned by the Royal Society for the Protection of Birds, bought with money raised by children of the Puffin Club (Penguin Books). These are the highest chalk cliffs in the country and the site of the only mainland gannetry in Britain.

June is the best month for seabird assignments. Eggs are hatching, chicks emerging. Outside the breeding season birds vacate the ledges to wander the oceans.

We parked the car at the end of Cliff Lane. As we walked towards the white chalk cliffs, a cacophony of sound greeted us: gruntings, trumpetings, squawkings, mewings, growlings. Then the pungent smell hit us, rotting fish and seaweed.

We stood at the railed-off observation platform at Bartlet Nab and looked down on to a spectacular scene. Rows of guillemots, densely packed, squatted on narrow sills. Most faced inwards, backs against the wind, nodding, bowing, dozing, brooding, shuffling webbed feet.

The chalk is flinty nearer the top of the cliff and weathers easily to provide niches for seabirds. Razorbills, less gregarious than guillemots, choose wider ledges on which to lay eggs, or retreat into narrow crevices. Puffins buzzed below us with short wings whirring, zooming out to sea and back, to disappear into holes in the crumbling top layer of boulder clay.

Guillemots are chocolate brown and white. Razorbills are *black* and white with deep, square bills. Puffins are, of course, quite unmistakeable, small and rotund behind the incongruously large striped triangular bill, with bright orange legs and feet.

We walked on, through a kissing gate, to Nettletup. On a guillemot ledge were two green eggs exposed to view. Broad at one end, tapering at the other, the shape guarantees that, if knocked, a harmless spin, instead of a disastrous rolling over the edge of the ledge is the result.

'A guillemot with specs on!' Five bridled guillemots stood grouped

'Seabirds on a chalk cliff.'

together. The curious fine white lines around the eyes resemble spectacles. A few 'bridled' birds are found in most colonies. One bridled gilly held his head high and with effort painful to watch, gulped down a long sand eel, head first. Auks are 'site-faithful', often returning to the same ledge and the same partner year after year.

Along the top of the cliff we walked. Fulmars planed below, stubby-necked, stiff-winged: a short burst of flapping followed by a long glide. They follow the line of the cliff edge closely and seem curious at the presence of humans.

At one nest site a pair displayed excitedly, preparing for a duty change. The off-duty fulmar had returned to relieve his/ her partner for a spell from the shared task of egg incubation. With wide open beaks both birds cackled – 'Kek-kek-kek-kek-kek-kek' – voices rising to an explosive crescendo. Sitting close, they threw back their heads and swayed ecstatically, a performance that precedes each shuffle on – or off – the egg.

We crossed over a stile. A cloud of small white gulls flew over our heads to land on the grass beyond: kittiwakes. Energetically, they plucked at the grass, tearing up beakfuls. Back they flew, beaks stuffed with this handy nesting material.

Kittiwake nests are extraordinary creations, hollowed cups of mud, grass and seaweed. Plastered to tiny projections on the chalk face, the majority survive howling gales and tempestuous spray-lashings. Tier upon tier of nests stud the chalk. An estimated 50,000 pairs of kittiwakes breed at Bempton – and thousands more breed elsewhere on Flamborough Head. Many of these nests now contained, in the month of June, sitting birds keeping their unhatched eggs warm. In other nests fluffy young flopped sleepily, or raised heads in hopeful anticipation of the next fishy meal.

'Kitti-wa-a-a-ake, kitti-wa-a-a-ake.' The plaintive calls echoed and re-echoed. In and out of coves flitted the gulls, small and pretty, with softly rounded heads and neat yellow bills. Triangular black ('dipped in ink') wing tips lack the white dot markings of larger gulls. Out at sea flocks hovered and plunged for fish.

We climbed one more stile. Three huge white birds flew low over the waves. We had reached the famous gannetry. On cliff ledges at 'Jubilee Corner' gannets sat in rows: white bodies, yellow ochre heads, glassy blue eyes, bluish-white dark-lined dagger bills. 'Urrah, urrah, urrah': their growling calls carried above the sound of the sea – and all those other bird noises.

Gannets were first recorded at Bempton in the 1920s and 1930s. One, sometimes two, pairs were reported. In the 1960s numbers began to increase, as they have increased in colonies elsewhere. Now the population estimate is around 650 pairs.

We stayed all day, suffering short drenching showers of rain and drying out in the hot spells in between. We climbed over more stiles and braved a herd of well-behaved bullocks. The sea below was so clear that it was possible to enjoy the underwater antics of swimming guillemots, even from such a height. The summery sound of a corn bunting's 'jangling keys' song followed us across the fields as, at day's end, we finally made our way back to the car.

Grassholm Island, Pembrokeshire, Dyfed

It was inevitable that, as I had stood watching the gannets at Bempton, memories of a visit to Grassholm came flooding back. We'd approached the remote, uninhabited Welsh island, twelve miles off the coast, in the *Cubango*. The steep, rocky prominence resembled a snow-capped mountain, so startlingly white were the birds and their droppings on top.

'Pooh, the stench!' we protested. Gannets circled out to meet us, black-tipped wings with a six-foot span beat the air with stately strokes. Hundreds sailed above our heads. Splash! Straight and swift they dived into the sea after fish, dropping like stones, torpedoing downwards. Up shot bursts of spray.

The water was green and glassy calm. One by one we clambered out of the boat and on to the slippery rocks of an inlet. Kittiwake noise greeted us. A small colony nested on the basalt rock face.

We scrambled to the top. Gannets, gannets, gannets. Thousands of the dazzling white birds were spaced across the summit in close proximity. Male and female take turns to perch on the bulky drum-nest of seaweed, incubating the single stained white egg. Hatched-out chicks, shapeless bundles of woolly white down, are fed regurgitated food from crops; small heads disappear into the gapes of parent birds.

There was much aggressive posturing, bowing, beating of half-open wings. Incomers landed clumsily and made their tricky way nestward; outgoers waddled to the edge of the rock and plunged seawards. Some were immature birds in brown and black speckled plumage still. The volume of noise was deafening.

We picnicked in a patch of golden samphire. A loud burst of singing gave away the presence of the ubiquitous wren. Dark rock pipits explored wet boulders. A surprising chaffinch flew down to peck at our crumbs. Thirty grey seals basked offshore. A nesting cormorant glared at us with green eyes, its black feathers glossed with a purple sheen. Two foggy-brown young hissed, and cowered nervously in their nest of dried seaweed.

The gannetry at Grassholm, with perhaps 22,000 pairs of birds, is an astonishing sight. Boat trips to the island are infrequent, possible only in perfect weather conditions. But the gannets of Bempton Cliffs are within easy reach of all.

J · U · L · Y

Fledglings – and Flowers

Wasdale Head, Cumbria

Wasdale Head boasts the highest mountain, the deepest lake and the smallest (although it is one of several claimants) church in England.

The road to the Head winds from the coast, past Wastwater with its forbidding scree slopes, to come to a halt here, thwarted by the Scafell masses in all their stern grandeur. Scafell, Scafell Pike, Great Gable, Yewbarrow, Kirkfell, Illgill Head: the place is a fellwalker's dream.

But I am not the most efficient of fellwalkers; others may go up top to conquer the summits; I prefer to wander in the dales. July, in the dales, is an excellent month for seeing 'summer' birds. Young have fledged. Families are flocking. The juveniles, many speckled still with yellow gapes, are unafraid. It is easy to stalk close, to enjoy their unashamed begging, their wing-quivering and plaintive cheeping – and the frantic efforts of parents to satisfy insatiable appetites. The young will not be pampered so for much longer but meanwhile, for the birdwatcher, it is an entertaining time.

I found myself not only enjoying the birds, but the flowers as well. It is our custom, as a family, to visit the Lake District in the peaceful, tourist-free month of October when campsites are uncrowded, autumnal colours of trees amaze – but flower presence is scant. But for once we had chosen mid-summer – and wild flowers bloomed in profusion. So I did not spend all my time peering upwards, searching the skies for those rumoured golden eagles.

The predominant flower colour was yellow. Yellow tormentil dotted the grass. Yellow pimpernel, dandelion, cat's ear, hawkbit, St John's wort and birdsfoot trefoil gilded the slopes.

Flowers – and fledglings. Young wheatears flitted across from the top of one drystone wall to another in front of me as I walked. Out of the corner of my eye I thought I saw a white butterfly – but it was the white pattern on the tail of an adult, checking up on the brood.

'Creamy honeysuckle.'

Two just-out-of-the-nest meadow pipits sat on a gate post. A parent bird flew down with caterpillar in beak. It must have been a very juicy caterpillar for, after satisfying the hunger of one offspring, several minutes were spent in fastidious beak-cleaning on a convenient patch of crinkly lichen.

Harebells – and sheets of yellow buttercups.

Three young swallows, palely coloured yet, perched precariously on a telegraph wire, wobbling, teetering, losing their grip, clutching again frantically. They could not have been long fledged; the white on their bellies still had a downy look. Handsome, glossy blue-black, red-throated, white-breasted, fork-tailed adult swallows dipped and twisted and soared, snatching winged insects from the sky and passing the insect 'packets' to their wire-clinging young. Sometimes the youngsters flew a few feet up into the air to take the offering – to return immediately to the safety of the wire.

A redpoll flock in a stand of willows, ruby-red foreheads glowing in the sunlight . . . young willow warblers calling softly, 'oo-ee, oo-ee' . . . midge-collecting martins . . . sky-scything swifts . . . meadow pipits, skylarks: there was no shortage of birds.

A common sandpiper bobbed on a boulder on the hillside, quietly piping, a muted whistle. As I neared it changed to a shrill triple 'peep-peep-peep'.

Heather, foxgloves, water forget-me-not . . .

Now I had reached the Wasdale Head Hotel. I crossed over the little pack-horse bridge. Challenging the fast-flowing stream, a black and white dipper 'swam' against the current, half-submerged as it snapped up aquatic delicacies. Then it flew to a boulder, blinked its white eyelids, bobbed and curtsied, and whirred upstream.

On the other side of the stream, against a background of creamy honeysuckle, a spotted flycatcher perched very upright, awaiting the unwary fly.

I walked on, following the windings of the splashing tumbling Mosedale Beck. Meadow turned to marsh. It was decidedly wet underfoot. I was glad of my stout walking boots as I squelched through boggy bits. Stretches of white silky-plumed bog cotton-grass and orange-yellow bog asphodel warned me to be wary.

I reached the desolate head of the valley (few flowers here) and decided to attempt a crossing to the other side of the beck so that I could return by the path descending from Black Sail Pass.

Clambering over rocks and following narrow sheep trails – which tended to peter out disconcertingly in the thick bracken – it took me a long time to find a possible beck-traversing spot. With nervous steps, I crossed from one sliddery wet boulder to the next whilst the water swirled and gurgled beneath.

I was nearly there – when I slipped! A wobbling of the stepping stone, a panicky leap – and I landed sprawling on a soft, spongy blanket of sphagnum moss: to find the fingers of my right hand touching a small plant – which I instantly recognised as the common sundew.

'It was a common sundew.'

I forgot my wetness, my dripping jeans, the soggy waterlogged ground. The sundew is a freak of a plant, a carnivore, which absorbs the protein in the bodies of its living victims. Round, spoon-shaped, reddish-green leaves in a rosette formation *glistened*. Tiny globular drops of a clear fluid tipped fine, red 'leaf-tentacles'. From the centre of the rosette sprang a single five-inch stalk with a small spike of closed white flowers at its end.

Growing in acid soil singularly poor in nutrients, it is remarkably adapted to obtain essential nitrogen from small invertebrates. 'Miracula naturae', they called sundew plants in the eighteenth century, and miracles of nature they certainly are.

I could see no creepy-crawly ensnared in the hairs of the Mosedale specimen. And squeamishness prevented me looking for a tiny insect to place on a sticky dewdrop leaf. But Dr A. W. Roth, a physician of Bremen, had no such qualms. He was the first person, so far as we know, to record the fact that the tentacles of the common sundew are capable of movement.

In 1799 he wrote, 'With a pair of tweezers I placed an ant upon the middle of the leaf of *Drosera rotundifolia* but so as not to disturb the plant. The ant endeavored to escape, but was held fast by the clammy juice at the points of the hairs, which was drawn out by its feet into fine threads. In some minutes the short hairs on the disc of the leaf began to bend, then the long hairs, and laid themselves on the insect. After a while the leaf began to bend, and in some hours the end of the leaf was so bent inwards as to touch the base. The ant died in fifteen minutes, which was before all the hairs had bent upon themselves.' (*The Carnivorous Plants* by Francis Ernest Lloyd, published by Dover.)

The rare great sundew and the rarer still oblong-leaved sundew, the common butterwort and the three species of bladderwort, can also be found in the wet places of the Lake District. All are carnivorous, insect-trapping plants: miracles of nature.

Shearwatering

Skokholm Island, Pembrokeshire, Dyfed

To ring Manx shearwaters, you need a lonely island, permission from the British Trust for Ornithology, a BTO permit and a good supply of BTO rings, a powerful torch, spare batteries, like-minded companions – and a plentiful supply of shearwaters.

Wait for a moonless summer night, or a night with a mere sliver of a new moon, and listen. If there are Manx shearwaters present on your chosen island, you will most certainly soon hear them. The noise of homecoming shearwaters beggars description: strangled gurglings, croupy gaspings, weird cacklings, raucous howlings; shearwater bedlam is indescribable.

In July and August, parents have chicks to feed. They fish at sea, following the shoals, and return to their burrows through the hours of darkness to regurgitate a fishy soup for waiting young.

Shearwaters are less vociferous on nights of the full moon and fewer return to the island – so, on a suitably *black* night, wrap up in warm clothes, shine your torch and head along the path which leads through scratchy heather, hummocks of thrift, and knee-high bracken, to the tussocky bumps of a cliff-top colony.

Thump! Thump! Thump! That's the nocturnal Manx shearwaters landing all around you, home again after many hours far out on the ocean. They must beware the huge beaks of the great black-backed gulls; turned-inside-out corpses and picked-clean bones on gull loafing grounds each morning tell a sad story.

Manx shearwater

Direct the torch and you'll find a bird. Black and white below, pigeon-size, smallish head, dark beady eyes, long wings tucked to sides. The thin hooked bill, with its external nostrils in tubes on the upper mandible, remind you that shearwaters are members of the strange 'tube-nose' petrel family.

At first the bird will be dazzled by the beam. Then it shuffles awkwardly on its belly towards its hole. Stoop quickly. Pick the bird up gently. But watch out for that stabbing bill.

Swiftly slip the numbered ring on to one of its legs. Adjust the thin metal strip with your special pliers. How far back the legs are set; ideal for swimming, but an explanation for its clumsiness on land. Now your bird is a numbered individual and, with luck, one day you may learn more of its history.

Release your bird. There is a hungry chick somewhere below waiting for food, a blue-grey powder-puff of a chick. Thump! Thump! Shearwaters are landing on all sides, filling the air with their strange cackling, gasping, whooping cries – and an oily musky smell.

Earlier in the evening you saw them floating patiently on the pink-tinged water offshore. In great pre-dusk 'rafts' they waited for the sun to set; or flew back and forth, veering from side to side. Showing first black, then white, they tip and bank and glide, close to the water, shearing the waves with long narrow wings.

The chick in the burrow below will now be guzzling the partly pre-digested fish food regurgitated by its newly ringed parent. For fifty days (an exceptionally long incubation period) it remained in the egg. Parents, on duty in turn, kept the egg warm and brooded the tiny chick for the first few days after hatching. Then it stays in the burrow alone, visited only at feeding times, for nearly two months. Fed on a diet of oily fish, it grows enormously fat.

Towards the end of September the adult birds begin their long migratory journey south across the Atlantic where they will winter in the tropical seas of South America.

The young shearwater finds itself deserted. After a few days of wing-stretching and flapping outside the burrow, it makes the perilous trip to the edge of the cliff. Flapping, scrambling over the rocks, it blunders its way to the sea. Then . . .? This is where our ringing comes in.

Clumsy on land Manx shearwaters may be, but they are elegant fliers and first-class navigators. One newly fledged youngster was found in Brazilian waters only seventeen days after leaving the nest.

Take a bird from its burrow in the breeding season and transport it to Boston, USA; release it – and it could be home in twelve days, given clear skies. Three thousand miles back home. You don't believe it? You must, it's been done, the numbered ring sufficient proof.

The young bird will wander the ocean and probably not return to breed for five years. It will then excavate a burrow, or take over a rabbit hole (ousting the occupant if necessary). Once it has chosen a mate, it will probably remain loyal to mate and to burrow for the rest of its life – and one ringed Manx shearwater is known to have lived for at least twenty-nine years.

Thump! Thump! Thump!

More birds, more shufflings, more rings to slip over the pink-grey legs with their webbed feet. Now it is past midnight. The eerie chorus shows no signs of abating. Sea noises fill the air. An oily fish smell fills your nostrils. There are stirrings over in the lesser black-backed colony, the lighthouse monotonously flashes its warning signals, Pauline's hot soup awaits you back at base – and you all agree: there is *nothing* quite like shearwater ringing.

Note: there is no longer a ringing station on Skokholm.

Seabird Sanctuary

Skomer Island, Pembrokeshire, Dyfed

We kept ourselves awake by playing poker dice by candlelight in the tiny kitchen. We had come to see the Manx shearwaters. Thousands breed on Skomer and the island is honeycombed with burrows. It was a long time since I had helped to ring shearwaters on Skokholm, another of the Pembrokeshire islands, and I wanted my children to see – and hear – the strange petrels.

Everything at first had gone according to plan. I put a call through to the West Wales Naturalists' Trust Office in Haverfordwest.

'Is it possible to spend a night on Skomer Island?'

Oh yes, I was told, providing we didn't mind tucking ourselves away in a converted cowshed. And using an Elsan. And fetching water from the well a hundred yards away. And boiling the water before drinking it. And becoming members of the Trust. And managing without electricity and plumbing. And taking enough food to last for several days in case the boat was held up by gales. And using sheet sleeping bags.

We didn't mind – and we booked.

We left Martin's Haven, near Marloes, on the morning of 4 July in the red-painted *Arklow*. A very tame herring gull perched on the rail throughout most of the crossing. Seaweedy coves, jagged spurs, narrow inlets and stacked rocks came excitingly into view.

'Poor things,' I thought, looking around at the other passengers and feeling superior. 'Mere day trippers, they are. Not island visitors like us.'

I looked smugly at my heavy rucksack with its bedding, iron rations, matches, camera, thick woolly, good torch, spare batteries, toothbrush, towel and soap. My binoculars I wore round my neck at the ready for all those puffins, razorbills and guillemots I expected to see on the way over. And did.

We landed on the quay of the three-mile-long island and were greeted by the Warden. He briefed us, and asked us to keep to the paths of the 'visitors' trail'. Tramping feet are a great threat to the vulnerable eggs and chicks of the central plateau.

For several hours we explored the island, two humps of rock, spectacularly eroded, joined by a narrow ridge. The clifftop turf was bright with thrift and sea campion. Many flowers of the heath grow on the central plateau. And there are marsh plants in the boggy bits and beside the little streams. It was a strange feeling when four o'clock arrived and the day trippers departed. As I had suspected, we were the only folk rash enough to have booked into a cowshed for the night.

Our quarters consisted of a row of cells, sparsely furnished, but clean. Some contained a single bed, others were twin-bedded. My daughter and I moved

'Remains of an ancient farm.'

into one and my son commandeered another. I was secretly glad to be sharing. The building was surrounded by spooky ruins, the remains of an ancient farm. The staff house was a mile away, on the Neck.

'I can't wait to see shearwaters again,' I said brightly to the Warden when he came to check that we understood about Calor gas, to remind us to boil the drinking water and to tell us the *exact* procedure of what to do if we fell down a cliff.

'Shearwaters?' he repeated lugubriously. 'Won't be many about tonight. Full moon, you know. Inhibits them.' (Oh dear, I had not thought to check the lunar date; how could I have been so silly?)

'Still, you might just be lucky,' he added. Then he headed for home. We were on our own.

We spent the evening at the Wick, looking anxiously at the fine, cloud-free sky; the moon had yet to rise and we willed a few obliging clouds to appear to block its light. We didn't spend *all* our time looking anxiously. The Wick is far too entrancing a place for that. It is a sheer basalt rock cliff on which thousands of razorbills, guillemots, kittiwakes, shags and fulmars nest.

Puffins zoomed around, skimming the cliff top, wheeling in great circles. Stalling, orange feet spread, they land with gentle thuds beside their holes. Picturesque in the pink thrift, gaudy striped bills crammed criss-cross with tiny silver sand eels, they pause, then disappear into burrows. My son's camera scarcely ceased its clicking. Comical rolling walk, pattering wing-flapping run, upright stance, growling call: 'Kaa-arr-arrr' – we could have watched them happily for hours.

But there were other birds too. The dark rock of the Wick was splashed with kittiwake droppings – streaks of whitewash – from countless cup-nests. Fulmars planed by on rigid wings. Guillemots and razorbills whirred rapidly out to sea, surface-dived for fish, and whirred back again to feed hungry chicks. We stayed until the sky turned to pink and the sun dropped below the horizon.

Before it grew any darker, we followed a little path to the well, a deep gap between boulders, and filled our kettle with water from the spring. Then we boiled it dutifully and heated our tins on the Calor gas stove in the kitchen. We squatted in the grassy compound and ate sausages and beans straight from their containers – to save washing up.

We threw grapenuts to the pigeons, and shooed the hens out of our bedrooms. Then we lit the candles and read the Visitors' Book through from 1960 onwards. Julian Huxley! Ronald Lockley! Tony Soper! Wow! How could we sign our own modest names after that high-powered lot?

By midnight we were all yawning hard and so I made some strong coffee to wake us up. Then we fetched our torches and, abandoning the cosiness of the kitchen, staggered out into the night.

We stood on the grassy (wretchedly moonlit) path and listened hard. Plenty of gulls still kicking up a shindy. There was a strange sort of hissing in the bracken to the west which I couldn't put a name to. The odd oystercatcher piped and a curlew called sleepily. Lapwings rose, flapped, peewitted plaintively and re-settled. But that was all.

'We'll walk towards North Haven,' I said. (I bet Tony Soper never gets the date wrong.) 'Masses of shearwater burrows in that direction.'

A moment later we saw . . . glow-worms! Tiny green balls of light phosphorescing at us from the dark of the bracken. Perfectly round luminous glimmerings. Dozens of them, on all sides.

We shone our torches here, there and everywhere. It is the female beetle (not 'worm') that lights up, to attract the male. Having no wings she can only crawl, so she stays put and 'glows' hopefully. When not lit up she is unlovely, flat and grublike. But on summer nights she lifts her 'tail' and on the underside of her abdomen are two tiny oblong patches of bright green florescent luciferin with reflectors of minute crystals. With these she signals, and a winged male makes all speed.

There are not many places left in Britain where glow-worm illuminations can still be enjoyed. Insecticides have wiped out most mainland colonies. (Snails should give thanks. Glow-worm young have a nasty habit of devouring snails – alive.)

We had wandered far from the old farm buildings. By now it was past one o'clock. Were the glow-worms sufficient compensation for the non-appearance of shearwaters? And then we heard them coming in: gaspings, crowings, croonings, cacklings. The sky had darkened, clouds had gathered, and birds were returning, flying in belatedly to feed their chicks.

We stood quietly, waiting. A thump close by gave me my chance. I shone my torch and caught a shearwater in the beam. We delayed it for only a moment or two, remembering the fluffy chick waiting below for its supper of regurgitated fish. But my children were as amazed at this strange petrel with its eerie call as I had hoped they would be.

Happily tired, we then crawled off to bed. And before I even had time to wonder if Tony Soper himself had slept between these very army blankets, I was asleep.

'Picturesque puffins.'

Choughs on a Cliff
North Pembrokeshire, Dyfed

The 168 glorious miles of the Pembrokeshire Coastal Path are tramped throughout the summer by 'backpackers'. With set faces, straining muscles, blistered heels, pedometers swinging from trouser belts, pockets bulging with maps and Kendal mintcake, and strict time schedules which must be kept to at all costs, they force themselves on, come gale, come deluge, come dehydrating heatwave. From our rented cottage on the north Pembrokeshire coast, not many yards from the cliff and the coastal path, we could see them; their youth hostel destination was at the end of our lane.

Backpacking is not for me. I don't care for Big Walks. I prefer Small Potters. The clash of ginger on pink as a small skipper butterfly lands on petals of campion; gorse pods popping in the hot sun; small striped snails creeping out on to the wet path after a cloud burst; soldier beetles gathered on the white umbels of wild carrot: these sights and sounds I can enjoy at my pottering leisure – whilst the hordes of laden hikers tramp by with stern faces and never a glance to left or right.

The Pembrokeshire Coastal Path was opened officially in May, 1970, after many years of tricky negotiations. It follows the cliff edge closely for most of its miles, from Amroth in the south to St Dogmaels in the north. Perhaps even more than most long-distance paths it deserves to be pottered.

The cliffs near our cottage, we discovered on the first day of that holiday, were wild and forbidding: of ancient, dark volcanic rock. Grey-wigged jackdaws with bright glinting eyes tumbled at the cliff edge. 'Jack, jack,' they call incessantly. But we were hoping for a much rarer black bird . . .

Offshore, fished arctic terns. They flit, skim, twist, squeal and squabble. With white plumage gleaming, terns hover, tails fanned, slim red beaks pointing down towards the water. Silver fish sighted, they brake; down they flash with closed wings. Upwards flies the spray as they slice the water and plunge beneath its surface.

On the cliff top, marsh orchids, pink and lush, clustered in damp hollows. Grasshoppers churred in the long grass. A handsome male stonechat surveyed the scene from its bracken perch.

We picnicked one day on a small secluded beach and, after, lay sunbathing on the hot sand. Screeching of terns, mewing of gulls – and the agitated twittering of sand martins. In and out of holes in the soft cliff face they darted: forked tails, sandy brown backs with a brown band dividing white throat and white belly.

Over the marsh stretching beyond the shingle bank at the top of the beach they hawked, snatching winged insects to carry back to their hungry young.

'Backpackers with set faces.'

The marsh was colourful with flowers; creamy-white meadowsweet, pink marsh woundwort, purple loosestrife. Mayflies and caddis flies were on the wing. Emerging damsel flies, a brilliant metallic green or electric blue, crept up long stalks to dry out.

Gnats swarmed above the marsh and the sand martins, twittering constantly, flew back and forth. They are opportunist birds, not wholly dependent on natural sites, but ready to take over man-made embankments. Quarry walls, drainage cuts, spoil heaps, road works, railway sidings . . . are sometimes colonised before the workmen at these sites (who mostly view the small birds with tolerance) have even packed up and left. Such embankments are often transitory structures, but sand martins, among the first of our summer migrants to return, are adept at seeking out the new season's workings.

The lane near our cottage led only to a farm, the youth hostel poised on the edge of the cliff and a monument to a Welsh poet, put there by his friends. In this quiet lane there was an extravagance of wild flowers, a riot of colour. I was reminded of John Barrett's eulogy in his book *The Pembrokeshire Coastal Path* (HMSO, 1974). 'Take almost any patch for exhibition at the Chelsea Flower Show and the rock garden medal would be yours!'

Sheltered from the wind by high stone banks, flowers grew in profusion in the lane. Tall foxgloves indicated an acid soil, as did wild thyme, sheep's sorrel, bell heather, tormentil and heath bedstraw. A few very late bluebells surprised; thrift and Queen Anne's lace were fading fast. The leaves of herb Robert were changing already to an autumnal red. But wall pennywort was a fresh green, and fresh too were the tiny pink and white flowers of English stonecrop.

Red admirals fluttered by – and there were other butterflies. Meadow browns, common blues and small coppers sipped appreciatively at nectar from creamy honeysuckle, white bramble and red clover. Speckled woods basked in the sun.

Ostentatious day-flying moths, the scarlet and black six-spot burnets, buzzed with whirring wings from yellow birdsfoot trefoil to blue sheepbit to mauve tufted vetch. We watched the emergence of one moth; it crept out from its pale yellow papery cocoon, and clung to the stem of grass to which the cocoon had been fixed with silken threads.

Above, in a blossom-burdened elder tree, redpolls called. The small flock of eight flitted before me along the hedgerow, drawing my attention to a white post in a bed of slender St John's wort and wood sage. It was discreetly positioned and bore the letters 'NR' painted on with white paint: NR for 'Nature Reserve'.

So our flowery lane was not our own secret discovery after all. Its worth is appreciated. An arrangement between the West Wales Naturalists' Trust and the Highway Authorities had ensured that the vegetation would be treated with the respect it deserves. No spraying, of course, and only circumspect cutting back at the most appropriate time.

The post was a challenge. Every flower must be identified! No problem. Proper potterers never travel anywhere without a botanising field guide in their rucksacks. Out came mine. Lady's bedstraw, bell heather, meadow vetchling, silverweed, eyebright, restharrow, hop trefoil, cut-leaved cranesbill, rock sea spurry, crow garlic . . . That lane was a delight.

On another day we climbed up the hill behind the cottage, a craggy natural fortress where Iron Age remains of habitation can still be seen, to look back from two hundred feet up. The coastline stretched away, hazy in the hot sunshine. In small fields, haymakers worked, perspiring with the heat. Deep fruity croaking – and a raven circled the fortress. 'Kronk, kronk.' We were

Bell heather

again reminded of those other black birds we'd hoped to find: choughs. Choughs are known to breed on Pembrokeshire cliffs in lonely caves and fissures, and on offshore islands. We scrambled back down the hill, avoiding gorse patches, surprising a wheatear.

A signpost pointed ahead to where the road rejoined the Coastal Path. We reached the edge of the cliff and flopped down on to the soft turf. Below, in a steep dark inlet, grey seals would pup in the autumn in the tiny inaccessible cove. The 'tseep-tseep' of a rock pipit echoed as it flew to a seaweed-strewn ledge.

'Chee-ow.' That was no jackdaw's call – although for just a moment I had taken it to be. I looked around. Again came the ringing call. Five choughs,

Wall pennywort

crow-size, glossy-black, hopped on the grass of a slope just below the edge of the cliff, digging curved beaks into the soil, ant-searching. Bill colour suggested a family party. The bills of the two adults were a brilliant red, matching their bright legs. Pale orange was the colour of the young birds' bills.

We sat very still. 'Chee-ow, chee-ow.' There are only a few coastal areas in Britain today still frequented by this attractive member of the corvine family. And it is the patient potterer, listening attentively for that twanging 'chee-ow, chee-ow' call, who is most likely to come across these secret retreats.

Pink Thrift and Puffins

Skokholm Island, Pembrokeshire, Dyfed

A day trip to Skokholm was included in the programme of guided walks organised by the Pembrokeshire National Park Authority, and we booked. I had holidayed on Skokholm many years before; I had even lived there for a while; the trip would bring back memories.

Skokholm is internationally famous as the site of Britain's first bird observatory, established by Ronald Lockley in the thirties. Lockley's original purpose was to farm the island but he became increasingly fascinated by its bird life; the books he subsequently wrote aroused interest worldwide. He organised the building of a Heligoland trap – a great wire funnel with a trapping box at its end – and he began to ring migrants. Ornithologists came to stay in the white-washed cottage. But the war forced Lockley to move to the mainland.

As soon as possible after hostilities ceased, the observatory reopened. Not long after, the Field Studies Council took on the administration. Today, the West Wales Naturalists' Trust shoulders the responsibility – and the Pembrokeshire National Park Authority organises occasional day trips.

The boat took us across from Marloes. Auks bobbed up like corks, tipped up – splash! – as we approached, and disappeared under water to swim easily with their small, pointed paddle-wings. Up they bobbed again behind us. Then the red sandstone cliffs came into view.

The lighthouse stood stark against the blue sky at one end of the island. Clustered at the other end was the white-washed observatory complex. The painted figure-head of the *Alice Williams* on her perch at the edge of the cliff; black cormorants gaunt on wet rocks; puffins standing sentinel on the slopes of Crab Bay; guillemots whirring over the sun-glinting water in follow-my-leader lines; noisy jackdaws stunting in thermals . . .

We landed at the quay in South Haven. Our guide led us up the winding path, past the old lime kiln, and across the Neck towards Stack Rock. Young oystercatchers with red bills still black-tipped; purple thyme and yellow tormentil; lapwings already flocking over on the Bog; skylarks singing madly in the blue above.

We headed for Purple Cove, passing on the way a hard-working party engaged in damming a stream to create a new pool for waders. Close by planed fulmars – newcomers since my last visit. Today there is a regular small breeding colony of this spreading species.

Another species which has increased dramatically is the lesser black-backed gull, to be counted now in thousands on the island's plateau. They flew up in clouds as we walked by North Pond, screeching at us and dive-bombing, protective for their chicks.

We picnicked above the steep red cliffs of Mad Bay and watched guillemots below on their ledges; and, higher up on the slope, razorbills with their downy young tucked away in niches under boulders. Yellow and orange lichens patterned the rocks and the cushions of thrift roofed burrows where nocturnal Manx shearwaters lay their solitary white eggs.

But time was passing. We cut across to the lighthouse with its helicopter pad and followed the old tramline track – past Sugar Loaf and South Pond, to Crab Bay with its puffins and pink thrift. Then a scramble up Spy Rock for a good view of the island. A curlew strutted below; it stopped, tweaked desultorily at a blade of grass, then flew off, opening its long curved bill to whistle, 'cur*lew*, cur*lew*.' Rabbits nibbled grass, wheatears clicked from the tops of stone walls, pied wagtail flew over: 'chissick'.

'Britain's first bird observatory.'

Following paths through the bracken, we reached the observatory buildings. Visitors come to stay here in the summer, sometimes for a week-long course in art or natural history; sometimes to follow their own pursuits. The famous Wheelhouse, mentioned in Lockley's books, is still dominated by the splendid brass wheel from the *Alice Williams*. The cottage looked cosy, with a driftwood fire laid ready and Tilley lamps waiting to be lit, to light up the common room at night. Drinking water is pumped up from the well in the meadow below, and cooking is by Calor gas – I know, because it was as bird observatory cook that I once spent eight memorable months on the island.

Skokholm is a good place to see migrating birds in spring and autumn. In summer time, the close views of breeding seabirds are the attraction. It is a much-studied small island, and all its wildlife, both fauna and flora, is of interest to naturalists and artists.

Skokholm Island

Birds are no longer ringed on Skokholm, but back in the 1950s, in the month of August, I helped to ring storm petrels. An estimated 6,000 pairs breed on the island.

I remember one such night. The moon was bright, casting weird shadows in the rocks, but we carried torches to light our path across the Western Plain to The Head. Sugar, the retired lighthouse stallion, was still alive then (he had an obituary in *The Times* when he died) and standing at a favourite spot in the Knolls. The flock of Soay sheep huddled close beneath Tabernacle Rock. Lapwings rose from the bog, screeched a protest as we passed, then resettled. Manx shearwaters vocalised from burrows. Rabbits paused in their

Soay sheep

nibbling, hesitated, then bunny-hopped to subterranean safety.

We set the mistnet up between rocks at the top of the cliff. From ledges below came groans of razorbill and guillemot – the few still in residence – most had already enticed their young down to the sea and were gone.

Storm petrels nest in crevices in old drystone walls built by the men who struggled to farm Skokholm over the centuries; or amongst boulder scree or rocky outcrops; or in old burrows, abandoned by rabbit, puffin and shearwater. We crouched out of sight, listening to the night noises and catching whiffs of the musky petrel scent. From holes came the purring of the occupants, 'Arrr-r-r-r-r-chikka'.

Beyond, the lighthouse beamed its warning flashes. Stars twinkled. The air grew chill. A slight breeze stirred. But the light nylon mistnet hung almost invisible.

Earlier we had seen storm petrel flocks flitting low offshore. Dangling legs patter the waves as birds hover and snatch surface food. As the last glimmer of the sun's rays fade, they begin their return home to lone chicks hungry for food. The young are fed, bill to bill, with 'regurgitated, predigested grey pulp'. The storm petrel chick is at first a tiny silver-grey ball of fluffy down. The rich oily diet of fish promotes a rapid weight increase and, two weeks before it leaves its nest, the fledgling is heavier than its parents.

The last half of July had been abysmally wet and windy that year, and some downy young must have perished, drowned by the torrential rain. Skokholm, which receives the full force of Atlantic westerlies, has the reputation of being 'one of the windiest places in Britain'. Sea mists are frequent – and the

126

lighthouse forlornly blasts its foghorn for hours on end.

But now it was August, the weather was fine and the air still. We watched the incoming of the 'stormies', dusky silhouettes in the moonlight. Winging erratically, they flickered their way to the rocks and stone walls, slipping through narrow cracks. Their flight is bat-like, silent.

Plop! A bird had slipped down into the loose pocket of the net. Gently Peter Davis (then Warden, and now an authority on storm petrel biology) lifted it out: small, soot-black, white-patched square tail. Like the fulmar petrel and the Manx shearwater, it is a member of the *Procellariiformes* – 'tube-nose' – order; fused nostrils on its hook-tipped beak form a tiny external 'tube'. Peter swiftly fixed the numbered ring to its leg – and it was released. Silently it flew to a gap in the stone wall and disappeared from sight.

Ringing these charming small seabirds identifies an individual, captures a moment in time. Recoveries are analysed and slowly facts emerge which build up a picture of its life history. Storm petrels spend most of the year at sea, wintering south of the equator. Young birds wander between colonies – but most return to the island where they were born, to breed in their fourth or fifth year. Couples remain faithful to each other, and to their nesting hole, and they can live for many years. Just a few of the facts which have come to light as a result of memorable moonlit mist-netting evenings on salt-sprayed cliffs – with the sound of the surging sea below.

Downy Ducklings
Arundel, Sussex

Photographing birds at a Wildfowl Trust Reserve is, perhaps, a bit of a cheat. But it is a great temptation to a beginner photographer, particularly at downy duckling time. Birds can be approached at such close range, and the surroundings are so near-natural, that satisfactory results are almost guaranteed.

I had only three hours to spend at Arundel with my Olympus OM 20. The light was right; now I must select my subjects.

A Bewick's swan was sitting on her tall mound-nest. But I had come too early; she was still incubating. An exciting event, said a Warden; exciting enough for the press to send a photographer along – if chicks hatched. Only a handful of the world's captive Bewick's swans have ever reared families.

Across one of the large central lakes sailed a flotilla of black-necked swans. Looming in the background above a canopy of trees were the battlements of Arundel Castle. It made a lovely picture, the Castle, the pool and the swans, and I clicked away.

Arundel

The tree-covered chalk escarpment of Offham Hanger dominates to the north of the reserve. Springs from the chalk feed pure water straight into the reserve ponds, an irresistible attraction for birds. I wandered along the winding paths which led past reedbeds and dykes, using up more of my film on a mother mallard with nine delightful ducklings. Tall reedmace ('bulrush') with brown velvety flowerheads, and clumps of comfrey, figwort and hemp agrimony made an attractive backcloth.

Canada geese paraded with gawky goslings running alongside: snap! Azure-blue damsel flies hovered: snap! A barnacle goose pecking vigorously at grain with its fluffy grey offspring pecking too: snap!

More excitement: a pair of trumpeter swans had produced five young – and this event had succeeded in making the headlines in the local paper. Trumpeter swans are a North American species which, not so long ago, was close to extinction in the States. Ruthlessly shot at on their long dramatic overland migration flights, their numbers dwindled. The threat was recognised in the nick of time and the swans are now protected by law.

The Arundel trumpeter swan family proved so photogenic that I had soon used up a film. I fed in the next one. Pen and cob alternated long rests on their island nest with gentle swims, escorting their frantically paddling cygnets. 'That's far enough for an early outing,' one could feel the pen thinking as they struggled back on to dry land, 'mustn't overtire them.'

I moved on, camera at the ready, and was soon admiring a photogenic goldeneye with a single duckling. A nestbox on a pole was their home. Goldeneye take readily to nestboxes in lieu of tree cavities. Swedish woodsmen found this out more than three hundred years ago. They introduced the practice, put up nestboxes – and ensured for themselves a supply of fresh eggs for breakfast. Nowadays commercial forestry with its quick turnover allows few holes in trees and so thousands of goldeneye nestboxes are positioned with conservation – not omelettes – in mind. The exercise has spread to Scotland and goldeneye now breed happily in Scottish forests. Before they are two days old, the young are enticed out of the nest by their mother calling from below. Thick downy fluff ensures a soft bouncy landing – although some must come to grief – and they are led away to a safe

'Tall reedmace with velvety flowerheads.'

'Photographing is a bit of a cheat.'

refuge. The nestboxes at Arundel are placed over water – and the ducklings enjoy a safe, if splashy, fall.

Most wildfowl young are self-feeding in a matter of hours. But on hearing a tiny 'squeak-squeak' coming from a gap in the emergent reeds, I peeped – to see a member of the rail family, a moorhen chick: a tiny bald-headed scrap with gigantic feet. Covered in straggly black down, with a wispy red fringe on its head, it crouched low, begging for food, squeaking, quivering, flapping tiny wings. Its harassed-looking parent dipped for green stuff and tucked a morsel into the wide-open orange beak, then dipped again.

Moorhens habitually produce two broods a year – and very occasionally three. Each brood can consist of up to ten chicks, and each chick wants feeding for up to six weeks. So it is as well that the first brood willingly helps with the rearing of the second. Close to an untidy nest of sticks constructed in the roots of a sallow tree, ungainly dingy-brown, almost fully-grown siblings were food-hunting that day to help feed their tiny brothers and sisters.

Time was passing. I hurried to a pool on which swam a number of familiar British ducks. Beside me, as I stood there, was a grandmother out for the day with her two young grand-daughters. They threw grain to the pintails, tufted ducks, shovelers, wigeon and pochards whilst I took more photographs.

The grandmother suddenly remembered that she, too, had her camera. She said brightly, 'I know, Caroline, we'll photograph you in front of the Carolina ducks, that would be nice. But where shall we take a photograph of Penelope?'

'In front of the Carolina ducks,' said Penelope stonily. But they were in for a disappointment. Carolina ducks, so exotic in their breeding plumage, are hard to find in the month of July. The drakes, resplendent earlier in the year, go 'into eclipse', skulking in the reedbeds and shedding their gorgeous feathers for dowdier plumage.

But I was never to find out where Caroline and Penelope eventually posed for their photographs. My three hours was up and, with four used films in my pocket, I had to leave. Arundel, open all the year round, is a peach of a reserve and a plum spot for photographers.

Aboard the Broads

The Norfolk Broads

We had hired a cabin cruiser. At first I feared we should have no time for birdwatching. It seemed to be all topping up, or pumping out, or manoeuvring for moorings, or negotiating rivers, or letting down the anchor (or pulling up the anchor), or mopping the deck, or foraging for food in the galley, or rescuing 'man overboard', or sailing the dinghy – but, of course, we *did* manage to birdwatch.

We boarded our boat at Potter Heigham and chugged off down the River Bure, mooring that first night below St Benet's Abbey. I tried not to think of the ghost as mists rose and swirled whitely over the flat cow pastures, and the pale shade of a predator barn owl wafted past our bows, and redshanks piped hauntingly from the fen.

St Benet's Abbey dates back to the tenth century. Two hundred years ago a windmill was built into the ruins. Now the windmill itself is derelict. It is too easy to imagine a swinging figure dangling at the rope's end from the great stone archway: the ghost of a treacherous monk.

Next morning the sun shone. Even more important, the wind blew. We could try out our little brown-sailed dinghy on South Walsham Broad, a mile away, up Fleet Dyke.

Greylag geese greeted us, honking with orange bills. Canada geese, with long black necks and white chin straps, grazed on the bank. A pair of great crested grebes, summer-ruffed and ear-tufted still, were doing a little out-of-season courting, head shaking, circling, ritually swopping gifts of green weed. Another pair on the same Broad were incubating. Their floating nest, anchored to the roots of a willow tree, was bulky, composed of waterweed and sticks. The grebe on guard slipped quietly under water as the dinghy neared; its mate sat tight on the eggs and we steered well clear.

Swifts soared spectacularly. Moorhens swam with jerky gait and disappeared into the reeds: 'Kr-r-r-rk, kr-r-r-rk.' Female mallards, a few inches of white-edged blue wing stripe showing against the sombre brown of plumage – as if a blue sash had been tied around their middles – dabbled at the water's edge.

Between us, we had scarcely any sailing experience. Luckily, the breeze was gentle and the water fairly calm. I held the rope (sheet?) in my hands, felt the wind tug at the canvas (mainsail?), got ready to dodge the pole (boom?) if it crashed (jibed?), gripped the steering lever (tiller? helm? rudder?) – and quoted all the John Masefield I could remember. The inevitable happened. A gigantic flap of the sail, a sickening swerve – and we were in the reeds. Stuck, and out of sight. Just me and the cabin boy.

'Our little brown-sailed dinghy.'

Over-confident, and attracted by a show of waxy yellow water lilies, we had unwittingly passed through the narrow channel which links the busy Outer Broad to the private Inner. We should probably be there still if a youth hadn't appeared in a small motor-powered boat; a Norfolk born-and-bred lad, very 'Big Six' and as self-assured as any of Arthur Ransome's originals.

'Lift centre board,' he advised tersely.

He towed us out into the middle of the water, gave a curt nod and brrrrm'd away. Crushed, we lowered the sail and *rowed* back to the cruiser.

My daughter was sitting on the deck, feeding the last of the Mother's Pride sliced to cute baby coots, little 'baldies', with the bare skin of their crown still a bizarre rose-red. Parent coots fussed attentively over their dependent young, tucking each breadcrumb neatly into the tiny red beak. Coot chicks, like moorhen chicks – and other members of the rail family – can be dependent on adults for food for several weeks.

We saw more birds next day on Salhouse Broad: black-headed gulls, shelduck, oystercatchers, lapwing. At Hoveton Broad we walked the nature trail; peat bog, fen vegetation and wet woodland. Duckboarding led us safely over (we were warned in our 'trail notes') treacherous liquid mud. 'The nearest thing to a tropical swamp you are likely to see in Britain.'

From an observation hide overlooking Hoveton Broad itself, we watched common tern fishing, red beaks black-tipped. House martins and swallows skimmed low. Reed buntings called, 'Chi-chi-chi-chitty' from a reedbed. Herons stood weirdly motionless in tops of trees. Early passage waders probed the muddy edge: spotted redshank, common sandpiper, dunlin. From alder and willow carr robins, thrushes, dunnocks, chaffinches, blackcaps and willow warblers sang snatches of end-of-summer song.

The Warden of Bure Marshes explained to us some of his problems of management. The natural advance of alder and willow must be kept in check or reedbeds will vanish and so, eventually, will the waterways. 'Man created the broads by extensive digging for peat in medieval times. Nature is determined to fill them in again,' he said. Sutton Broad has already gone.

So British Trust for Conservation Volunteers chop down advancing trees and shrubs, harvest the reed and sedge, mow old meadows to improve ground flora and tend the rides to encourage orchids. They coppice alder for broomheads and clean out turf ponds to tempt back otter, kingfisher, dragonflies and the swallowtail butterfly.

The main waterways have, for some years, suffered from a surfeit of nitrogen and phosphates; nitrogen-rich run-off from the surrounding agricultural land, combined with effluent from sewage treatment works containing high concentrations of phosphates. These two chemicals act as plant fertilisers and the abnormally high levels have resulted in a super-abundance of algae which 'take over' the water, depleting the oxygen and

Canada geese

making it difficult for aquatic life to survive. Aquatic plants have disappeared in many areas; little animal life remains, apart from the ubiquitous tubifex worms and 'bloodworm' midge larvae which contain haemoglobin in their blood and can live on in the oxygen-depleted mud layer.

Pressure on the Broads is colossal. Two thousand boats a week are hired out each year during the April to October season and the majority of these are cabin cruisers. Over 7,500 privately-owned boats are licensed to use the waterways.

But steps are being taken to 'clean up' the water. The Broads Authority is pumping out the offending mud. The Anglian Water Authority 'strips' phosphates at source. And the Norfolk Broads has been designated 'an environmentally sensitive area' (ESA). Farming threats have included the ploughing up of grazing marshes for arable; the reseeding of old sward; and damage to reed fen by lowering water tables. Now farmers are encouraged, through the ESA compensation scheme, to use farming practices which protect the delicate ecological balance of the Broads – the last stronghold of a wealth of plants and animals.

But many acres of the marshes and broads are already managed by conservation bodies: the Norfolk Naturalists' Trust, the National Trust and the Royal Society for the Protection of Birds.

At Bure Marshes corrugated iron barriers have been experimentally fixed at the point where the reserve's dykes meet the river. Their purpose is to keep out polluted water. Behind these barriers, rarer species of plants, said the Warden, are returning to the clean dykes.

Hornwort is the first to appear; it springs up from seeds which have lain dormant for years. Soldier flowers are good indicators of pure water. Bladderwort, a 'carnivore' which traps and ingests small crustaceans in tiny bladder-snares; floating frogbit; holly-leaved naiad; bur reed with spiky fruit resembling the ball-and-chain weapons of medieval knights; these are some of the interesting plants which have recolonised the clean water.

With the return of the plants, come insects. We found a fussy freshwater bug, the water-stick insect. It breathes through a snorkel-like tube at its 'tail' end and is an excellent indicator of pure water. Two inches long, brown, with hidden-away wings, its front legs are equipped at their tips with grasping organs; it feeds by piercing its prey and sucking out the juices with modified beak-like mouthparts.

Damsel-flies – 'flying darning needles' – flashed blue-black across the water and pond-skaters skidded over the surface.

Dykes were originally dug with access and drainage in mind. They also served to prevent cattle from straying. Marshmen kept them clear by constant 'dydling' with long-handled scoops. But that was long ago. For years dykes have been neglected and allowed to silt up – or drastically over-deepened and cleaned out by heavy machinery with no thought for wildlife.

'Foxgloves had opened their mitten flowers'

At Bure the compromise is to use a 127mm Sykes Univac Pump once every ten years; it sucks up the mud Hoover-like and jets it on to the adjacent fen with the minimum disturbance to flora and fauna.

Now we wanted more sailing. The windmill-lined River Ant wound its tortuous way to open out into the enormous Barton Broad. Banks of purple and yellow loosestrife fringed the water's edge and a hawker dragonfly darted – hovered – darted. In spite of all the demands put upon it, Broadland is still beautiful. We let down the mud-anchor and took off in our dinghy. This, after all, was where Nelson learnt to sail.

(above) Meadowsweet; (far left) 'Whiskery cascades of old man's beard' and purple loosestrife; (left) Slender St John's wort

Noctuids for Nightjars

Holme, Norfolk

Moths are a popular prey item with many bird species – according to the *Birds of the Western Palearctic* (edited by Stanley Cramp, published by Oxford University Press).

The stone curlew catches moths in the air 'by running chase and jump'. The merlin hunts by 'short-distance surprise attack' and day-flying moths 'may form substantial part of diet of young . . . in years of special abundance'. The little ringed plover sometimes 'hits the moth against hard substrate before swallowing'. Occasionally a curlew on the ground will snatch a moth from the air and 'larger insects may be squashed between mandibles'.

Hobbies are known to eat moths in flight, 'when caught in open sky'. Golden plover, kestrel, coot, whimbrel . . . are on record as moth eaters.

The nightjar is especially adapted for nocturnal moth catching. It has an exceptionally wide gape fringed with prominent rictal bristles which unfold to form a natural trap as it hawks low. On a nightjar's middle claw is a 'comb', used – so I read – to groom its bristles free of moth scales.

And many more species of birds feed on moth *larvae*.

I saw my first 'setaceous Hebrew character' at Holme Bird Observatory in Norfolk. It was a pale fawn moth with dusty pink and black hieroglyphics (the 'Hebrew characters') on the forewings, and it had been lured by the light of a mercury-vapour lamp. It nestled in a hollow in a sheet of egg-packing material, just one of the 380-odd species to have been trapped, identified and censused by the Warden of the Bird Observatory. For over twenty years, Peter Clarke has been recording the moths of Holme. At dusk, he releases the day's catch, unharmed, from the collecting box.

The purpose of our visit to Holme was – to watch birds. But when we were offered a demonstration of the live moth trap, we abandoned the small flock of pied flycatchers in the sea buckthorn and joined others eager to view the night's catch. In papier-mâché nooks, moths were sleeping the daylight hours away: angleshades, rustics, wainscots and a nice frosted-orange – as well as the setaceous (meaning 'bristly') Hebrew character.

More moths for me not long after, at the edge of a Leicestershire spinney at 9.30pm on a summer's evening. It was nearly dark. An overcast sky, no moon or stars, a warm and humid evening. 'Just right,' said an old hand.

We switched on torches and followed our leader into the dark of trees, past a stream, reedbeds, willow and alder, hawthorn and meadowsweet. Now we were blinking in the brilliant light of a mercury vapour light bulb suspended from a stick tripod. On the ground beneath was spread a large white nylon sheet. A flex ran from the bulb to a purring generator beyond.

We settled ourselves around the sheet and talked in whispers, faces purple and macabre in the artificial light. Experienced moth trappers were the ones equipped with extra clothing, portable stools and hand lenses.

'Looks as if it's going to be a good froghopper night.' The only creatures so far to be seen on the sheet were tiny 'cuckoo-spit' bugs. They were congregating in dozens to trampoline on this surprising new surface.

But an hour later the moths were coming fast and furious. Baffled by the light, they were easily caught and popped into small transparent boxes, to be passed round the circle, identified – and released into the outer darkness. By the light of torches Richard South's classic volumes on *The Moths of the British Isles* were perused, matching scale pattern to picture.

At first all moths looked confusingly alike to me, until I realised that many species are dubbed with helpful descriptive names: double-square-spot, heart-and-dart, marbled-beauty, twin-spot-carpet, shoulder-striped-rustic, lunar-spotted-pinion, the spectacle (this last had two black rings – 'spectacles' – on the front of its thorax). So many moths with so many subtle variations in scale patterns – 'as if programmed by a giant computer,' said Ian.

One of the first to arrive was the 'drinker'. It flew dizzily into the circle, a large ginger-brown moth, the intruder with the crazy drunken flight which whirrs around bedrooms on warm summer evenings – to the consternation of wouldbe sleepers. (The drinker caterpillar is reported to *drink* drops of dew clinging to leaves.)

A moth like a small white feather, fluffy, with a silken sheen, landed on the sheet. 'Don't touch!' The yellow hairs on the tip of the yellowtail's abdomen, used by the female to protect and disguise her eggs, can cause nettlerash in a human.

More moths dropped on the sheet with gentle thuds. ('Another one of *those*'; we were becoming blasé.) The magpie-moth was orange-banded and black-spotted; its lurid coloration warns birds of its nasty taste. Chinese-characters at rest (wings closed) uncannily resemble bird droppings, a weird disguise which, presumably, protects against predators. The snout was an odd looking creature, with enlarged palps elongating its head shape.

Light-arches and dark-arches are 'nothing to get excited about' – but a *buff-arches* is 'something else altogether' it was agreed; fancy-patterned olive, orange and white.

The beautiful yellow-brimstone, the delicately pink-spotted peach-blossom, the common-white-wave with its whiteness broken by fine wavy grey lines, and the neatly marked clouded-border, were treats.

White-ermines, white and furry, had wing borders dotted with tiny black spots. A yellow-underwing at rest was stout-bodied and sober-coloured – like most 'noctuids' – but when it took off in sudden flight, underwings flashed brilliant.

'There's another footman.' Footmen can be recognised by their stiff 'livery-clad' appearance; they hold their long narrow wings close to the body.

July-highflyers were common. They are members of the 'geometer' family, the caterpillars of which arch and loop as if 'measuring' the ground: 'inchworms'.

Purple-thorn . . . scalloped-oak . . . dingy-shears . . . the engrailed; by midnight we had caught, identified and released over fifty of the 2000-plus species to be found in the British Isles.

'Pass that to the 'pug' man . . .'

'Nice pyralid, who wants it?'

'Let's lose this micro . . .'

Micro-moths are mostly minute and difficult to identify. But not all are 'impossible'. The gold-fringe was bright pink with a yellow border; a scalloped design marked the wings of the mother-of-pearl; white patches on the very narrow forewings identified the grass-moth.

It was time to go. I stood up and shook myself, and out of my hair and clothes tumbled more moths. I was very stiff, my left leg had pins and needles, the air had grown chill – but for a learner lepidopterist, it had been a most rewarding evening.

Terns Scolded Us

Gibraltar Point, near Skegness, Lincolnshire

The adult education department of the University of Nottingham was organising a course for parents and children at Gibraltar Point Field Station. This time I would be able to take my two youngest with me. We were promised general natural history – with plenty of birdwatching.

Adults and children were to work in separate groups, receiving separate tuition. Parents watched with easy minds as children vanished after breakfast in the morning. Knowing them to be safe, busy and happy, we could relax and enjoy our studies. And study we did.

Out on the saltmarsh we studied vegetation. Succulent, salty *Salicornia* (yes, it was Latin nomenclature before many hours had passed) springs from

seeds embedded by waves in bare, black mud. Covered by sea at every tide, it helps to check the water flow, to collect silt – and to extend the marsh. *Salicornia* (glasswort, sea samphire) we decided, is the pioneering plant that gradually raises the soil level and allows sea meadow-grass, sea spurrey, sea aster, rice grass, the aromatic sea wormwood and the beautiful sea lavender to colonise and spread.

Small flocks of skylarks and meadow pipits rose, swirled – and resettled on the saltmarsh before we had time to reach for binoculars. Once grounded, they were hidden from sight as they searched for seeds. High up on the saltmarsh greyish-white plants of sea purslane fringed the channels – 'crab grass'; shore crabs take advantage of its shelter. A twittering party of linnets, a sprinkling of goldfinches and a squad of plain brown starling youngsters rose in clouds, eddied – and settled again.

We walked back past the muddy creek and put up a redshank: 'Tyuuuuuuu, tyuuuuuuu'. Two ringed plovers continued to patter and probe, leaving tiny footprints in the wet mud. A pied wagtail strutted along the bank above.

In the sandhills we examined the beginnings of a tiny dune, noting how the flotsam of the strand line – torn-off seaweed, dried-up seamat, papery beige ball-clusters of whelks' egg-cases, skates' egg-cases ('mermaid's purses'), the cast-off shells of crabs sun-bleached to whiteness, human litter – acts as a windbreak and collects blown sand. The sand is trapped – and a dune begins to form.

First sand couch grass moves in, sending out its underground rhizomes, putting up shoots, trapping and binding and compacting the sand. It prepares the way for marram grass and the beautiful blue-green lyme. As the dunes become established, other plants creep in: hawkbit, sorrel, sea holly, storksbill, sand spurge, birdsfoot trefoil and the useful mosses and lichens.

At Gibraltar Point, sea buckthorn has invaded the oldest ridge of dunes. In summer this dense prickly shrub provides shelter for the nests of whitethroats, sedge warblers, linnets, redpolls, dunnocks and yellowhammers. In autumn, its orange berries attract the thrushes: fieldfare, redwing, blackbirds, ring ousel, song and mistle thrush.

We left the dunes and, traversing the sandy shore, moved out on to the mudflats. There, we took up our spades and dug. A great tripper-attraction we were this sunny August day as, mud-besmeared, we discovered wriggling bristle worms and pink-shelled Baltic tellins and fan worms in delicate mosaic-patterned tubes of shell fragments and sand grains.

Terns scolded us, cockles squirted at us and shrimps adroitly dodged our swishing nets.

One of the few freshwater ponds still to contain a puddle of water in the heatwave conditions was a thick, concentrated soup of swimming, wriggling, jerking, burrowing, lurking aquatic creatures, into which, next day, we curiously dipped. Trays of water stood ready. We turned our nets inside out and watched fascinated as the containers suddenly became alive. We got down on our hands and knees to do some sorting out.

The great water boatman (or backswimmer) quickly made its presence felt. Hairs on its abdomen trapped air bubbles and its back was boat-shaped with triangular markings. It shot from side to side of the container – but upside-down, hanging from the surface of the water, spying on possible prey beneath with large back-of-the-head eyes. It is a greedy carnivore and chases after its victims with powerful strokes of its long, hairy, paddle-like back legs and then gets to work with its biting, sucking mouthparts. The great water boatman was hard to ignore – but its cousin, the lesser water boatman, swam convention-fashion, right way up.

Freshwater worms emerged from the silt and wriggled energetically in S-shaped curves – or jerked with a telescope-like movement, stretching and contracting.

'Leeches,' gasped someone as little lumps of black jelly arched along, gripping with suckers, looping, gliding. And freshwater snails crawled along the side of the tray.

From the weed emerged insect larvae. It was difficult to believe that these uncomely creatures were destined to become, in brief adulthood, beautiful winged mayflies, dragonflies and damselflies.

Back at the laboratory we sketched, made notes and peered down microscopes. Minute 'thingies' miraculously grew a hundred times as great. We gaped at the throbbing of a water flea's heart, at the neat green egg-sac of the one-eyed *Cyclops*, at the slim tail filaments of mayfly larvae, at tiny spider-like red mites, at minute bean-shaped Ostracods, at worms so transparent that their guts showed rather rudely, at eyes on stalks, feathery gills, biting jaws . . .

Satisfied at last, we released our booty back into the pond, hoping they hadn't minded too much. Then, from a distance, we watched the return of the five dunlin and two little stint we had frightened away.

And the children? They had a wonderful time. They chased each other with the prickly fruit of burdock, hunted in the ragwort for cinnabar caterpillars, dug for lugworms, feasted on ripe dewberries and tangy glasswort, learned to mimic the shrill piping of the oystercatcher, watched a greenshank from the hide, played rounders in the evenings and swam.

They sketched from the banks of the River Steeping, watched the boats sail in with the tide and made collections of snail shells. They painstakingly excavated a seven-foot root of marram and chopped it into lengths at the knots to show annual growth rate. They drove the Heligoland trap – and caught three meadow pipits and a reed bunting. They plotted and surveyed and followed a nature trail and answered quizzes. They talked to us expertly of long shore drift, neap tides, habitat recorders and belt transacts.

Alec Chater, their tutor, they told us, was 'dead knowledgeable'. 'Brian Thompson's dead knowledgeable, too,' we replied, 'and not only that – he's also adept at putting the kettle on at pleasurably frequent intervals.'

It was good to find that other people's children, as well as mine, lost their combs and *never* closed doors; good for my children to learn that other children's parents, too, insist on the necessity of boring routines like washing and going to bed.

Parents and children ate meals together, and walked together in the evenings to watch the tide sweep in over the saltings, and the wheeling clouds of waders, and the gulls on the shingle spit.

A Kestrel Hovered . . .

Slapton Ley, Kingsbridge, Devon

A kestrel hovered, side-slipped . . . hung low, with scarcely a flicker of feathers. We were close enough to see the barring on the chestnut plumage and the black tail band. Female. No slatey-blue on head or tail.

We were camping just down the road from the Slapton Ley Field Centre (one of the nine centres owned by the Field Studies Council) and I'd joined a 'Slapton Safari', a weekend non-residential course.

On Friday evening, those of us on safari climbed into a mini-bus and drove to Start Point. The track from the car park to the lighthouse is a well-trodden one, but we turned right to join a less frequented coastal path along the top of the cliff – and that is when we saw the kestrel.

Twelve-year-old Andrew dived into the grass after grasshoppers. He caught one – green as the grass – amongst the moon daisies, wild carrot, yellow agrimony, purple thyme and pink thrift. He held it in cupped hands. We gathered round to admire it – and it leapt high and escaped.

I found a bloody-nosed beetle. In the palm of my hand it oozed drops of 'blood' from its joints; a most effective 'defensive mechanism' for I quickly let it go!

A dark rock pipit was snapping up insects with its thin pointed beak. Shags preened oily-green feathers below the narrow path where the cliff dropped to a steep rocky cove: top-knot crests ruffled by the wind, gaping beaks outlined with yellow. White droppings on the cliff face showed the site of a nest. With quivering cheeks two youngster shags peered up at us, rasping their alarm. A stonechat, in the bracken behind us, clicked its disapproval – and we moved on.

Next morning we drove to Prawle Point. In the back of the mini-bus was a collection of shrimp-nets, buckets and plastic bags. The programme, said Peter Holden, was to investigate the zonation of a wild and rocky shore.

At the top of the shore, high tide level and above, was the 'lichen zone'. Patches of crinkled lichen, grey, orange, brown, yellow, dark green – dry and brittle to the touch – encrusted the rocks. Scavenging sandhoppers plundered the rotting jetsam and tossed-up sun-dried seaweed of the strand line below.

In the 'littoral zone' of the middle shore boulders were draped with green and brown wrack seaweeds. Clinging to the fronds we found creatures equipped with moisture-preserving shells ('life-support capsules,' said Peter) and so adapted to withstand long hours of exposure as the tide ebbed and flowed.

The limy plates of acorn barnacles were tight-shut. Periwinkles, topshells and dog whelks were safely sealed into shells with a horny plug (operculum). The limpet clamped itself to the rock strata with its powerful muscular foot, its shell a perfect fit. Bivalve mussels, fastened by tough threads to the rock, pulled both shells together. Tube-dwelling worms backed down into their neatly constructed, purpose-built tube-burrows. Beadlet anemones, blobs of dark jelly, contracted to save moisture in the dampness of a crevice.

'A shag with top-knot crest.'

But further down were deep rock pools in which the now-submerged anemones had opened to loose sticky tentacles, and to sway them softly in search of prey. If my gently probing finger had been a straying shrimp, the tentacles would have instantly engulfed it, stung it to oblivion with tiny darts, swallowed it down into the gaping mouth/stomach.

Rock pools, as every child knows but which I, sadly, had almost forgotten, are entrancing places: bright green sea lettuce, delicate red-tinted tufted corralines, chalky barnacles with feathery 'feet' protruding, transparent fish, scuttling crabs, tiny shrimps.

Simon bent to pick up a fragile brittle star. Carefully he held it in the palm of his hand. It slowly and laboriously turned itself over, shedding bits which it would later regenerate. We followed with our fingers the track where a grazing limpet had rasped algae cleanly from the rock with its toothed radula (the small muscular pad which is its feeding organ).

We put names to the tangled seaweeds: channelled wrack, spiral wrack, serrated wrack, and bladder wrack – (and the children were soon 'popping' the bladders). Then we moved on to the 'laminaria zone' exposed only when the tide was at its lowest – and Peter had timed our visit right. We waded in gullies, our wellies flagellated by tough leathery oarweed with a salty tangy smell. Great branching holdfasts anchored long blades of the weed to the ancient volcanic rock.

'The oarweed will eventually be torn away by the force of the waves, its holdfast taking with it a chunk of rock,' pointed out our leader, 'an example of biological erosion.'

In this most exciting zone, exposed only for a short time each day, we searched for sea creatures. Slimy orange sponges, encrustations on the rock, feed by drawing in water through minute pores, filtering off edible particles and then blowing out the water and waste through small communal openings. Seen close up, through hand lens, we decided they looked like miniature volcanoes. A dark blue colonial sea squirt, daintily white-patterned (daisies? stars? snow-flakes?) was pronounced by Peter to be a star-ascidian sea-squirt. It felt jelly-like and squirted at us – but we agreed it was a very pretty thing.

The blue-rayed limpet is also a little beauty; its delicate luminous kingfisher-blue rays looking as if they had been painted on the semi-transparent shell with the finest of paintbrushes. A young specimen (for, as the limpet grows older, the 'rays' fade) it was feeding in the hollow of a branching holdfast.

But the children liked best the velvet swimming crab. It glared fiercely at them with bulging red eyes and lunged with threatening claws, the crossest crab I have ever seen.

'Last time we came on a Safari, Alan picked one up,' challenged Diana. Thus dared, our leader courageously tackled the crab. The bravest of us stroked the purple, velvety-feeling back. Its legs were handsomely marked with well-defined black lines and blue joints. It protested strongly, and we let

145

it go and watched it scuttle away into the dark of a cranny.

Colin, a keen member of the Young Ornithologists' Club, was constantly on the look-out for birds. There were plenty of gulls – herring and black-headed – scavenging on the shoreline. Oystercatchers vigorously attacked mussels with their stout, chisel-bills, prising them open, snipping the adductor muscle. Out at sea, a young learner gannet, in first year dark plumage, was making a clumsy job of fishing; time and again it dived – and missed.

It was time to go. We hoped we'd left the scene much as we'd found it. The children nagged us.

'Put that stone *down*, dad, *gently*, *just* as it was; it's their *home*.'

'You've held that long enough, it needs water, it'll *die*.'

'*Don't* drop it, it's a nice crab.'

We returned to the field centre for an evening of natural history films – and then it was back to my tent at the campsite. I awoke next morning to heavy rain and had to splosh my way through puddles to meet Peter. Shore work was out of the question, we all agreed sadly. Instead, mackintoshed, we walked on Berry Head, identifying Devonshire flowers of a limestone cliff. And Diana made pets of striped snails, watching them with fascination as they crawled along the wide sleeves of her orange cagoule.

Spoonbills

Minsmere, Suffolk

Two spoonbills stood motionless, heads tucked under wings, long legs knee-deep in water. We watched them from the Island Mere Hide. We hoped they would stir themselves for we wanted to see those singular spatulate bills.

A shoveler flew by with a flash of blue forewing: green/white/red/black bands across its under-carriage.

A last few avocets remained to impress, birds of delicate beauty. It had been a good breeding year for avocets.

Clamorous black-headed gulls . . . ragged lapwing flocks . . . scurrying ringed plovers . . . common sandpiper with 'white shoulder straps'.

'Bittern,' exclaimed someone unbelievingly, and we watched as this most secretive of birds revealed itself in a short flight past willow scrub. It rose up out of the reeds, neck extended, long legs trailing, big owlish wings: a bulky golden-brown weirdo of a bird. It flew low, just a few yards, then dropped back down again into the reedbed. And still the spoonbills napped.

It wasn't until a female marsh harrier sailed above, and then flapped leisurely and low over a spread of pink marshmallow, that the two visitors stirred. They stretched their long necks, preened, and then, stiff-legged, swooshed the tips of their bulbous spoon-shaped bills through the water, sweeping from side to side.

We had arrived at Minsmere, the Royal Society for the Protection of Bird's Suffolk Reserve, early that morning. Permits are issued on a 'first come, first served' principle so that at no time is this popular reserve uncomfortably overcrowded. With its seashore habitat, shingle, freshwater lagoons, mudflats, reedbeds, islands, deciduous woodland and surrounding heath, it attracts over two hundred species of birds each year, and 95–100 species stay to breed.

August is the time to see migrating waders on passage. Their short breeding season is at an end and they are on their way south. We went first to the Scrape, an area of large shallow lagoons and small islands. It was artificially constructed in the 1960s, and so successful has it been that this prototype is a standard conservation measure in other wetlands, both in Britain and abroad. The water is fairly brackish and rich in invertebrates such as shrimps and midge larvae, the food of waders and their chicks. De-luxe one-and-a-half-decker hides offer birdwatchers excellent views.

Three little stint were running to and fro in the reeds. Very active, V-pattern on backs, smart little waders from the far north, High Arctic birds which breed on coastal mainland tundra and on islands, they were now heading for warmer wintering grounds. The little stint is neat, precision-perfect. It looks as if it is machine-made, with every feather meticulously in place. Swop a feather here or there – and it would make no difference. Chestnut coloured in spring, it is a sombre grey in late summer, on passage.

Plumage change is the factor which makes identification of small waders outside the breeding season such a challenge. Gone are the easily distinguishable patterns and colours of summer. We all know that at least 90 per cent of small waders at a pool will probably be dunlin but, once the smart black belly patch has vanished, there isn't a birdwatcher alive who won't try to turn the grey-brown ubiquitous bird into something more 'exciting'.

Dunlin are noticeably hunch-shouldered, short-necked, dumpy. The tip of the bill is slightly down-curved and there is dun grey speckling on the throat. But every birder still hopes. *Could* that dunlin on the left in truth be a semi-palmated sandpiper? a Temminck's stint? or – even – a short-billed dowitcher???

A dozen dunlin followed now, after the little stint, hurrying, busily drilling beak-prod stitch-marks into the mud. We were able to make useful comparisons.

Beyond these s.l.j.'s (short-legged jobs) a godwit probed: long slightly upturned bill, long legs. But black-tailed or bar-tailed godwit? The *black*-tailed looks as if it will stand smartly to attention if you bark 'shun'. It is tall and lanky and softly patterned. The *bar*-tailed, on the other hand, looks bar-backed – as if someone has run his fingers through the feathers from head to tail, leaving ruffled striations – and it is stockier, less graceful. The wader took off. It swept across the lagoon, tail black-banded and wings a dazzling pattern of black and white zigzags. 'Weeka-weeka-weeka,' it called – yes, we were right, a black-tailed godwit.

A spotted redshank, dusky black in early summer but pale grey and white now, high-stepped through the water to join knot and ruff. Knot? Plump, over-fed looking birds. Ruff? Disproportionately small head to body.

We moved on, walking through woodland: more birds. We climbed the steps to the tall Tree Hide – and watched dragonflies through our binoculars; enormous specimens were to-ing and fro-ing over dykes and pools. Swallows circled and soared, 'Squeep, squeep, squeep', across reedbeds and banks of hemp agrimony, purple loosestrife, codlins-and-cream willow herb, marsh sowthistle – flowers in their prime in the month of August. More sightings of a marsh harrier; legs trailing, undercarriage down, it came in to land – and we moved on to the Island Mere.

To reach the hide we followed a path through dense reeds. We could hear the 'fairy cash register' call, 'pching, pching', of bearded reedlings. We watched for the small buff bodies with the violet-blue heads to jet-streak out with long vapour-trail tails following after – and were rewarded with brief – too brief – glimpses.

And then, from the hide, we saw the spoonbills.

Spoonbills are an endangered species in many areas of their range. Small colonies are scattered throughout Europe and Asia. They have not bred in Britain since the seventeenth century and Minsmere would like to entice them back. These two young birds could be wanderers from Holland where about 200 pairs breed each year. Might they be prospecting? Sussing out a site? Avocets, ruff and black-tailed godwits have returned to breed after many years of absence; why not the spoonbills?

Spoonbills require seclusion, dense reedbeds, shallow unpolluted water with a soft mud base, and small fish and aquatic insects to feed on. All this the Royal Society for the Protection of Birds provides at Minsmere. So maybe next year . . . ?

Spoonbill

Twitching

North Norfolk Coast

'Twitchers' are birdwatching enthusiasts so consumed by the desire to acquire new species for their lists that they are prepared to travel almost any distance for the coveted 'tick'.

Each spring and autumn there will be birds on migration which lose their way and, especially if weather conditions are adverse, will end up far from their planned route. Birds from Eurasia and birds from the Americas 'turn up' in Britain – to excite the twitchers. Sadly, it is probably true that few of these exhausted off-route accidentals manage to survive for long.

Some orthodox ornithologists look down upon twitchers. 'Tearing around the countryside . . . list tickers, that's all they are . . . might as well collect car numbers.'

And, just occasionally, twitching comes into disrepute. There are stories of heartless chivvying of a rarity, of damage to a farmer's crops, of disregard for a landowner's property. Only a tiny minority of birdwatchers may misbehave – nevertheless, the editor of the twitchers' favourite monthly magazine, *British Birds*, decided the time had come to draw up a 'Code for Twitchers'.

One August morning early, a small group of us gathered in the middle of town all prepared to role-play at being twitchers ourselves. Where rarities lurked, there would we go.

'We'll be model twitchers,' we agreed sheepishly, clutching our 'species check lists'. 'We'll stick to the code. No harassment. No disturbance. The welfare of the bird comes first. Promise.'

It was 6am. What news from the grapevine? 'Not-a-lot-about,' said our contact. But contacts always start off like that, continuing with, 'Now *last* week . . .'

'There's a white-rumped sandpiper at Cley,' he went on. ('If you are among the first to hear of a rare bird, satisfy yourself that the site can cope with the likely influx of observers before spreading the news,' cautions *British Birds*.) White-rumped sandpiper – exciting; and Cley Marshes can cope with an influx of twitchers. But would it still be there?

'We'll stop at Titchwell Marsh on the way,' we said. We knew the route well. ('Before setting out, ensure that you are fully informed concerning how to reach the site.' *BB*.)

As we drove off in a light drizzle, a splendid rainbow appeared in the sky. Promising better weather, and glimpses of white rumps?

'It should be renamed *Twitch*well,' muttered someone, a few hours and a number of most rewarding sightings later.

August is the peak month for wader passage. Grey plover (still in summer plumage), turnstone, dunlin, spotted redshank, greenshank, ringed plover, ruff, snipe: we ticked them all off. Three black-tailed godwits stood with beaks tucked under wings, then roused themselves to drink, scooping up water with their bills – and slurping most of it out again.

A common sandpiper piped piercingly as it flew the length of a dyke. We soon spotted a curlew-sandpiper. Its white rump caused a momentary flutter, but its down-curved bill put us right. Next, a green sandpiper; snow-white belly, dark breast, dark greenish above – and, yet again, a conspicuous white rump. 'Too-leet, too-leet,' it called as it shot up in alarm.

That wasn't the end of the sandpipers. A 'woodsand' appeared, doing a lily-trotter, seemingly walking on water (actually treading across a surface layer of green algae) on long yellowish legs. And a purple sandpiper: yellow legs, plump, dark plumage – with no trace of white.

We reached the sea. Not once had we left the official paths. ('Do not try to get closer than anyone else to view or – especially – to photograph the bird: let binoculars, telescopes and telephoto lenses cover the distance,' states the Code.) We'd seen no-one behaving thoughtlessly. ('Never turn a blind eye to any misdemeanours committed by others.' *BB.*)

The beach was open to the general public and a man walked his dog. A hunched group of oystercatchers piped their agitation, red bills pointing to the ground. Twenty-three eider ducks rode the waves. Terns (little, sandwich, common) screeched and dived after fish. And girl bathers cavorted – fair-breasted sandpipers? – and we discreetly trained our binoculars elsewhere. ('Be tactful, informative and friendly,' urges *British Birds*, 'towards non-birdwatching onlookers or local people'.)

Back down the path we walked, past lagoons, reedbeds, woodland. More migrants: turtle dove, yellow wagtail, cuckoo and wheatear . . .

On to Cley-next-the-Sea. 'Anything about?' we asked after parking the car dutifully in the official car park. ('At the site, park sensibly and safely, follow up any instructions responsibly.' *BB.*)

To our delight, 'White-rumped sandpiper off the Iron Road.' ('If you pass on the message, do so carefully and in full.') Our quarry was still around and, most conveniently, it had chosen to settle outside the permit-holders-only zone. We could hardly believe our luck.

The sun was shining now, the wind had dropped and the light was good. Sea lavender in bloom. Yellow-horned poppies. A painted lady butterfly.

A long line of telescopes and binoculars jutted from the sea wall closest to us. Behind, and well out of sight, a row of birdwatchers peered discreetly. Twitchers all, perhaps, but not the uncaring sort that the editor of *British Birds* has to compose codes for. Experienced twitchers, maybe? ('Especially if you have previous experience of visiting rare bird sites, offer advice on any special arrangements which may need to be made, and offer on-site assistance if you are able.').

The bird posed nicely. Remaining in the same patch of shallow water, it pattered and probed for food. Sometimes it preened, offering hints of possible whiteness. Dunlin-sized, short straight bill, short legs, long wings projecting beyond tail, ash-brown plumage. Now it flew a short distance. And – there! the white rump! Muted sighs of satisfaction all round. It really was a most considerate bird.

Why all the twitcher excitement? The white-rumped sandpiper, unlike the other sandpipers we had seen that day, is a North American vagrant. It breeds in Arctic Canada and should, by rights, be wintering in South America. At the end of summer it puts on large fat reserves and flies out to sea to head non-stop down the western Atlantic seaboard to south of the equator. But a rapidly moving depression can sweep the birds across to Europe – and on to the lists of British twitchers.

Time was getting on. We should have to go. The white-rumped sandpiper seemed settled; it had found a spot which suited it – and suited its watchers, too. ('Be patient and restrained, especially if the bird moves suddenly to a new site nearby: give time for a new plan to be devised to cope with the situation,' advises BB.)

We decided to make a quick detour to East Road to see what other birds were around, keeping to the paths, closing gates. ('Observe the Country Code at all times.') A stunning avocet with three young in tow. Piratical skuas gull-chasing. A kittiwake circus offshore. Gannets fishing far out. Tick, tick, tick, tick.

We drove home, tired but triumphant, gathering a few more ticks on the journey. Then we counted up. Sixty-three different species. The white-rumped sandpiper was a lifer for us all. I had two more lifers beside. How about that for a good day's twitching?

Firecrest Finale

Gibraltar Point, Lincolnshire

It's up before dawn for a keen ringing group. Whilst it was still dark, we set up the mistnets in the sand dunes. Prickly sea buckthorn was smothered with orange berries, vitamin-rich food for incoming thrushes. We hoped for a 'thrush rush'.

We lay low and waited. The four nylon nets hung still, almost invisible, for there was scarcely any wind. Rabbits returned to nibble within a few yards of us. The sea fog slowly lifted as the sky lightened. We could distinguish the throaty calling of skylarks, the twittering of linnets, the ticking of robins, the chooking of blackbirds.

Autumn, like spring, is 'all change' time. As the first of the fieldfare and redwing fly into Britain for the winter, the last of our swallows, martins, chiffchaffs, wheatears and all the other little summer visitors are departing, 'exchanging their seats according to season,' wrote Sir Thomas Browne, a seventeenth century naturalist.

Three centuries on we waited to see which birds were 'exchanging their seats'. Clear skies and a north-easterly wind the night before would have tempted them to risk the sea crossing. But drizzle and mist in the early hours had forced them to land on reaching the Lincolnshire coast. Shadowy shapes flickered past us; possible chats, possible finches.

Ringers train for many months in the field, receiving tuition from BTO experts. Their skill and expertise must be of a high order if they are to rate the award of ringing permits from the British Trust for Ornithology. Without such permits, ringing wild birds is against the law.

A linnet was the first catch. With the greatest of care it was removed from the pocket of the nylon net into which it had slid, to be 'processed'. The 'biometric data' would be noted on the record cards. Sex? Juvenile or adult? Wing length and bill length? Weight? Out came the scales and the ruler.

The group had brought along its own portable box of BTO equipment. The box contained reference books, rings of all sizes, pliers, a pesola spring balance and plastic cones for weighing, a perspex ruler, calipers for measuring, BTO moult record cards and a log book.

'Prickly sea buckthorn smothered in berries.'

The ring is a thin, very light strip of metal. It bears a unique number. Once it has been positioned on to the bird's leg, a point of time and space in its travelling has become an established and proven fact. Follow-up data is of very special value. And so light is the ring that the bird is unlikely to be aware of its presence.

Softly blowing into the feathers revealed those missing due to moult. How many primaries and secondaries had been shed? How many replaced? How many were 'in pin', ie about to grow? The BTO wants to know. Statistics collected are systematically fed into the BTO computer at the BTO Headquarters in Tring. About half-a-million birds are ringed each year and annual recoveries average 13,000. Ringers have their own bulletin and they meet regularly at conferences and write papers for *Bird Study*, the BTO Journal.

Organised ringing began in Britain in 1909. Millions of birds have been ringed since. A vast data bank of complex material has accumulated. Movement studies depend on ringing returns and so, increasingly, do the life histories of individual birds. Ringing reveals weight fluctuations, the pattern of pair bonds, moult procedures, longevity and cause of death of different species.

As the mist continued to lift, and to drift away across the sand dunes, more birds flew into the nets. Quickly they were released: skylarks, meadow pipits, chaffinches, greenfinches, blackbirds, starlings. The morning passed, it was time to eat. We took down the nets, had our lunch, and decided to take a look at the Heligoland trap.

We crossed the saltmarsh to reach the great wire funnel, twenty foot wide at its entrance and sixty foot long. The funnel, set over vegetation attractive to small migrants, narrowed to a wooden catching box. We walked through the funnel – and up flew three skylarks and a meadow pipit – into the catching box.

Later that day we reset the mistnets close to a woodland pond. Seeding thistles tempted a charm of goldfinches. They snipped the blowing fluff, and probed the seedheads with sharp beaks. We caught nine: bright red faces, brilliant yellow wing stripes, tinkling calls. We ringed, released – and off they flew, back to the thistles.

Now three swallows perched on the top strings of one of the nets. They were juveniles, this year's youngsters with an over-all tatty 'unfinished' look and they had yet to grow the fine tail streamers.

I held a dusty-pink long-tailed tit in my hand. Its eyelids were *orange*, giving the eyes an orange-rimmed appearance. A few minutes later, a brambling revealed that, beneath its wings, axillary feathers are a startling *lemon-yellow*.

The afternoon began to close in. We caught our hundredth bird. It was a third ring ouzel, a female. She was a mottled greyish-brown colour, but feathers were fringed pale cream, a scalloped 'lace' edging. The crescent on the breast was scalloped too, a creamy-buff, not white as on the male.

It was time to take down the nets. Just as we unpegged the last of the guys, there was a flick! – and a tiny exquisite bronze-coloured bird with a yellow and orange crown, black eyestripe and white 'eyebrow' flew into the net and squeaked, 'Zit, zit, zit'. A *firecrest* finale.

Kingfisher with BTO ring

'Coulda Beena . . .'

Wells and Holkham, Norfolk

'Yellow-browed warbler sighted on the North Norfolk coast,' reported the Rare Bird Alert System (c/o 'Nancy's caff'). Last seen, Wells-next-the-Sea. The strong south-easterly wind had swept the tiny Asiatic warbler off its Siberia-to-India migratory route.

Birds were on the move. Some, the-all-the-year-round residents, would not travel far. Others had long journeys to make. High up in the canopy of the pine trees planted to stabilise the sand dunes at Wells was a spotted flycatcher. It darted out and back, feeding diligently to store up enough energy for the arduous flight south. A coal tit hopped up the trunk of a pine, investigating insect-concealing fissures in the flaky grey bark. Flocking blue tits, great tits, goldcrests . . .

Over our heads flew a great spotted woodpecker in dipping woodpecker-flight: three or four quick wingbeats followed by a long bounding swoop, wings held close to the body. Conspicuous with its bold colours – pied black and white with red on the nape and red under the tail – it bounded away into a thick stand of conifers.

A pied flycatcher was feeding among the needles. Two green and yellow siskins searched for tiny winged seeds of female catkins in a silver birch, acrobating with agility among the twigs. Brief snatches of song signalled the whereabouts of a female blackcap; between phrases she was enjoying ripe blackberries. And a blackbird, too; purple blackberry juice stained his yellow beak. (In the brambly sandhills of Holme Bird Observatory further along the coast, humans are sternly forbidden to eat the juicy fruit. 'BLACKBERRIES ARE STRICTLY FOR THE BIRDS' reads the notice.)

Marsh (or willow) tits flickered in and out of the tangles of brambles. Tits can be berry-eaters as well. Marsh or willow? The black crown of the willow tit lacks the rich gloss of the marsh; and the edges of the willow tit's flight feathers are milk-white, giving the appearance of a pale patch on the wing. But differences are so slight they are rarely of use in the field. 'If it calls, "Pitchew" – it's a marsh tit,' said Chris.

Not all birds are berry or seed eaters (although many species, particularly the thrushes, are able to change to a vegetarian diet – as insects, spiders, slugs and snails become winter-scarce). A redstart posed with sprightly upright stance and quivering chestnut tail. It held a red admiral butterfly in its beak – another little insect eater.

Redstarts were common that day. We saw them ground-feeding amongst the fallen pine needles, stoking up with 'fuel' for the next stage of their long-distance flight to West Africa: fuel in the form of energy-producing food. A

155

body-enveloping layer of fat is vital to migrating birds, conditioning the distance which can reasonably be flown to the next refuelling stop.

Pied flycatcher . . . wheatear . . . willow warbler . . . redstart. Wells-next-the-Sea is as good a place as any to view small summer migrants resting. feeding, waiting for a favourable wind to help them across the Channel and south to winter quarters.

But – no sign of the yellow-browed warbler. The willow warbler had caused a momentary stir, raising our hopes – only to dash them again by giving us a clearer view. Our commonest and most widespread migrant, its pleasant dying-fall song would be heard no more until April comes again. For a small bird it possesses surprising stamina and journeys to its wintering grounds in tropical and southern Africa in gigantic long-distance hops. 'But it *coulda beena* yellow-browed warbler,.' we agreed sadly. We were to see many more coulda-beenas that day.

We were looking for a tiny greenish bird, not much bigger than a goldcrest. Its underparts are white, faintly tinged with yellow, and over the eyes are the yellow 'brows'. Creamy wing-bars are another diagnostic feature.

The path led over the dunes to a wide stretch of beach and the sea. House martins swooped after midges on the edge of the dune ridge. Offshore, gannets fished. A redshank lifted its leg to scratch and its silhouetted reflection shimmered in the water of a pool. Cormorants wing-stretched in a steep-sided channel. A kittiwake patrolled the shoreline.

We met other birdwatchers. 'The yellow-browed warbler has moved on to Holkham Gap.' We walked back past the lake, pausing to watch a little grebe chugging its way from bank to bank, stopped to point out a parrot crossbill, silhouette unmistakeable, in a conifer – and then hurried on to the car park. To see still more birds.

High on the dead branch of a pine perched a kestrel, quite motionless. Black-headed gulls squabbled over a discarded sandwich. And in a patch of yellow ragwort, tweaking the petals of flowerheads for possible beetles, was a whinchat. It had its back to us, revealing a rich scaly pattern of black and brown feathers. At the base of the tail were two small white patches. The bird turned its head and showed its bold eye-stripe. Whinchats, unlike stonechats, are migrants. Longer wings enable them to cover greater distances. Whinchats may risk the perils of the journey – but stonechats suffer the hardships of the British winter.

We drove on to Holkham village and down Lady Anne's Road. The car park attendant was busy. Rumours of a rarity must make a considerable difference to his takings for the day. Holkham is a National Nature Reserve, the largest coastal NNR in the country. It extends from Burnham Overy to Stiffkey, an exciting area of dunes, saltmarsh, pools and reedbed.

A path led the way through trees and shrubs changing to autumnal colours, from greens to yellow, orange, brown and crimson. A late grayling butterfly flickered by. Shrubs were berried: blackthorn, rosehip, elder, hawthorn, honeysuckle. Starlings, blackbirds and song thrushes fed greedily.

It began to rain. Sheltering under the trees we watched more redstarts and blackcaps in the elder and bramble which fringed a reedbed and pond. A wren 'tick'ed' very loudly close by.

Raindrops set leaves trembling. Ever optimistic, and twitchingly alert, we deluded ourselves that each leaf tremble *could* have been caused by a foliage-gleaning yellow-browed warbler. The rain stopped, but the tantalising leaf trembling continued as drops gathered and plopped. Arms began to ache from the constant lifting, focussing, and lowering of binoculars.

Gusts of wind sent leaves flying – another tease. Each twirling leaf raised our hopes. It coulda beena . . . But it wasn't. We met other birdwatchers, equally bemused.

So we gave up. We decided to forsake rarity-hunting and to enjoy unstintingly all those other splendid little travellers which had dropped in for the weekend. And that is what we did. Our last memorable sighting of the day was a redstart bathing in a trickle of rain water.

Harbour Haven

Pagham Harbour, Sussex

The county of Sussex has the most built-up coastline on the south coast. Thanks to a young soldier fighting the North African campaign in World War II, there is one oasis where it is still possible to escape the crowds and to enjoy the peace and quiet of saltmarsh and sea.

Michael Alford, in 1943, wrote home saying how splendid it would be if, after the War was over, Pagham Harbour could be preserved as a haven for wildlife. His suggestion spurred local people to form the Pagham Harbour Preservation Committee and, in 1964, the West Sussex County Council declared it a nature reserve and took on the management. Its boundary is followed by a public footpath which offers good birdwatching.

Autumn is a good time to visit Pagham Harbour and we booked into a hotel at Selsey. Strangely, the best place to see interesting waders on passage is in a pool close to the busy road which runs behind the Harbour. Rarities have a habit of 'dropping in' for a few hours at Ferry Pool, and it was to Ferry Pool that we hurried first thing next morning. But other birdwatchers were before us, telescopes trained on to a lone wader which stepped delicately on long slender pale-olive legs, its graceful shape reflected in the still water. In contrast to the white belly and grey speckled back, its breast was a warm-pinky beige.

'Wood sandpiper', everyone agreed, 'juvenile.' It was a good beginning to the weekend.

Feeding in the fields beyond was a scattering of black-tailed godwits and a flock of fifty ruff. In the shallows of the pool, close under the bank: spotted redshank and two juvenile little stint.

We drove to the car park at Church Norton and walked through the churchyard to the little Chapel of St Wilfred. Inside the Chapel a stained glass window depicted wildfowl and waders of the Sussex coast – brent geese, shelduck, golden plover, curlew, avocet and oystercatcher – all birds we had a fair chance of seeing over the weekend for, we had learned, already the wintering brent geese were flying in.

Birds were not the only creatures featured in the ancient Chapel. Rudyard Kipling once visited, and the poem he afterwards wrote, based on a Sussex legend, is on display. It tells of Eddi, the Saxon priest, and of the Christmas when 'Nobody came to service/ Though Eddi rang the bell. "Wicked weather for walking," said Eddi of Manhood End, "But I must go on with the service/ For such as care to attend".' And, in the best tradition of Christmas tales, an ox and an ass 'pushed in through the open door'!

No oxen or asses around today but the trees of the churchyard offered shelter to small migrants. A bright redstart perched on a tombstone, then flicked its chestnut tail and darted grasswards to snap up an insect. A chiffchaff hopped through the branches of a yew and a blackcap briefly showed itself.

We passed through the porch and walked on down the lane which led to the harbour, pausing to admire delicate flowers of pink centaury and a healthy patch of yellow fleabane. On the shingle beach there were more flowers: yellow-horned poppies with crinkly petals and the long sickle-shaped seed pods, cushions of sea campion and the sticky, well-named 'stinking groundsel'.

We settled ourselves on the shingle and looked across to the area where little tern nest in June. The area is roped off for a few summer weeks and sympathetic holidaymakers are happy to stay clear. It was near here, one windy night in 1910, that the spit was breached and the sea broke through, flooding the land which Victorians had so painstakingly reclaimed. The gale was described by the local Vicar at the time as 'one of the most terrific hurricanes in the memory of man'. There has been no attempt since to enclose and drain the old harbour for agricultural use. Instead, its value to wildlife is recognised.

Scanning the wader-packed mudflats through binoculars, we picked out redshank, dunlin, godwit, turnstone, grey plover. Then – excitement! – a sparrowhawk swept dramatically across and panicked the flock into swirling flight.

A trudge across the shingle brought us to the path which skirts the saltmarsh and leads to Ferry House. On the saltings grew more flowers; lush spreads of rice grass with spiky flowerheads of creamy-white woolly stigmas; succulent glasswort in autumnal shades of orange and red; sea purslane with mealy grey-green leaves; mauve-petalled sea aster; and – a real treat – tiny shell-pink blossoms of sea spurry.

Ripe blackberries grew on the embankment to the landward side and soon our fingers and mouths were stained purple. A mink showed itself briefly. Silk nests full of tiny caterpillars . . .

Later we drove to the Visitors' Centre and followed the old Tramway, which for forty years, linked Chichester and Selsey. A dozen eiders bobbed on the rising tide and terns squabbled and fished – until a dark-phased Arctic skua swooped in and caused havoc with its piratical hassling. A streak of brilliant colour – and a kingfisher flashed down-channel to land on a wooden post. Boldly patterned shelduck paddled in the wet mud of channel banks; a small skein of brent geese flew over; the evocative calls of redshank and curlew fluted across the harbour; and a heron headed for home.

Next day we began our walk along another stretch of harbour perimeter at Sidlesham Quay. The old mill pond was in the process of being dredged. We got talking to the owner, who told us that it had not been cleaned out for some years. She planned to create islands to make it more attractive to nesting birds. Cargo boats had carried grain and coal up the deep channels to Sidlesham until the middle of the nineteenth century and thrilling tales are told of smugglers and wreckers and excise men.

'The wood sandpiper went on feeding.'

Past the 'Crab and Lobster' to shortcut across a field. Goldfinches flitted ahead of us along the blackthorn hedge – and the gorse and barbed wire fences were alive with whinchats and wheatears.

We reached the raised Pagham Wall, an artificial bank reinforced with wooden ramparts and stone facing, a defence against the highest tides. On one side lay mudflats and waders, and on the other – a reed-fringed pool. We watched the pool for a while, and were rewarded. Coot, moorhen – and a water rail which stalked between the reeds and emerged boldly for a few minutes, giving better views than this secretive bird usually allows.

A small thatched building, thought to be a seventeenth-century salthouse connected with a local salt panning industry, marked the end of the Pagham Wall. And almost the end of our autumn break. We returned to Ferry Pool, we hoped for one last sighting of the wood sandpiper – but it was gone. Disappointed, we were about to depart. Then 'It's flown to the little pond behind the Centre,' said a passerby. And it had. And so tame was it that it seemed oblivious to our circumspect approach and quietly went on feeding in the water beside an old rowing boat – and was still there when, regretfully, we really *had* to go.

Stormy Weather
Titchwell Marsh, Norfolk

Titchwell Marsh, on the north Norfolk coast, is another RSPB success story. Since its inception the number of breeding species has shot up from 39 to over 70. Bitterns now boom. Marsh harriers have bred. Avocets successfully rear young. Spoonbills settle for days. Black-tailed godwits linger in autumn in increasing numbers. Hen harriers roost in the reedbeds.

It is the introduction of new habitats which has attracted the newcomers: a freshwater marsh, a freshwater reedbed and a brackish marsh. On each of our visits over the years we have noticed changes; signs that the imaginative and ambitious plans for the reserve are paying off.

The Royal Society for the Protection of Birds bought the land in 1973. It was then an area of saltmarsh, shingle beach and sand dunes. The RSPB wanted greater variety. The addition of freshwater and brackish water areas would attract a whole new range of invertebrate colonisers which, in turn, would attract new birds.

So an army of volunteers went to work. Sea walls were built to cut off 100 acres of saltmarsh, and a system of dams, sluices, ditches and pipes was created to provide for the regulation of water flow. The construction of large hides with the best possible views followed, for the declared management policy was to make the reserve better for terns, waders, wildfowl, reedbed birds . . . and people.

We were grateful for the shelter of one of these new hides on our most recent visit, one day in September. The sky was ominously dark as we parked the car. A storm was brewing. We walked through a plantation of fast-growing trees. Planted to screen the car park, visitors' centre and toilet block, these trees also provide nesting sites for passerines. And, curiously, they attract some of the more unusual migrants. Hoopoe, golden oriole, black redstart, ring ouzel, Cetti's warbler and red-backed shrike have all been seen within yards of the Centre.

We reached the reedbed at the start of the long West Bank which leads from Centre to sea. Here we paused, to binocular-scan for bearded reedlings. Most of the reedbed, formerly tidal, has been converted to freshwater – and the reedlings prefer it that way.

Norman Sills, the Warden of Titchwell, makes clear in his book, *Titchwell, the First Ten Years*, the extent of the task undertaken. The long seawall, New Bank, was built in sections. Dragline machines gouged out a calculated 100,000+ buckets of mud from the saltmarsh to create this bank. To protect it from the force of the sea, 6,000 disused polythene sacks were collected from local farms, filled with sand by volunteers, and 'dragged through mud up to position on the polybag wall where they were laid down, kicked, flattened and sworn at'!

Frustratingly the sea broke through twice, bags were scattered and the work had to begin all over again.

But it was eventually completed – and one result is that part of the extensive reedbed is no longer tidal. Fallen reed-litter, the preferred nesting material of reedlings, is no longer washed out to sea at each tide. Neither is it jam-packed into tight wedges. It lies, undisturbed, in a loose, deep layer. Numbers of reedling pairs are increasing; they build nests of stalks and leaves on the litter layer.

Bearded reedlings are resident birds; they are locked into a reedbed existence, feeding on insects in summer and seeds in winter. But we didn't have time after all, to reedling-watch that day. Suddenly the clouds burst, thunder rolled, lightning flashed, rain sheeted down – and we ran for the cover of Parrinder Hide.

Settling ourselves on the benches, we peered out. Rain coursed down the glass of the windows, obscuring our view. In spite of the cold northerly wind which was howling straight off the sea, we were forced to open the windows and endure the blast if we were to see any birds.

What would their reaction be to this sudden downpour?

The hundreds of hirundines, hawking for tiny midges, gradually abandoned their efforts and disappeared – into the shelter of the reeds.

Ringed plovers, at the edge of an island, continued for a while to feed. They move as if working out a dance routine: step – step – step – step; bob, peck, pause, turn, step . . .

Dunlins, too, defied the storm and carried on feeding, a mechanical 'stitching', d-d-d-d-d-d. But both ringed plover and dunlin had, eventually, to admit defeat. The plovers crept into the shelter of weedy vegetation on the island and the dunlins waded out into the water and just stood there, hunched up, 'bewildered', visibly flinching.

Stop-and-scan-and-bob lapwings took off for inland fields. Shelduck squatted stoically, heads turned, beaks tucked under wings, raindrops rolling off oily feathers. Defeated redshanks flew towards the sand dunes.

But another bird which also appreciates the presence of midges breeding in their millions continued to feed throughout the storm: a black tern. Its graceful swooping, twisting, side-slipping hover-dip manoeuvrings were wonderful to watch. In the early years there were only occasional reports of this small, slim, slate-grey and black tern at Titchwell. Now they arrive on passage every year to feed, before continuing on their way to West Africa.

The rain stopped. We left the hide and followed the bank, the freshwater marsh to our right and grazing marshes to our left. The level of the water on the freshwater marsh is kept low in autumn to attract passing waders. Seventeen species are regularly seen, feeding in shallow water and on the exposed mud. In winter, the depth is increased – to attract ducks. Back flowed the swallows and martins from the reedbeds. Gnats danced again in dizzy swarms. A heron flew in, hopeful for a freshwater eel or two. A black-tailed godwit probed deep, submerging its head completely. Little stint, curlew, sandpiper, whimbrel, turnstone . . .

Sea aster bloomed mauve, its petals sparkling with raindrops. A bedraggled wheatear stood in our path, feathers awry, too miserable to hop out of our way until the last moment.

We reached the brackish marsh. Fewer insects breed in brackish water, but oppossum shrimps and ragworms – much beloved by the 'sweeper' birds, avocets and spoonbills – are plentiful. Lapwing, wigeon, gadwall, pintail . . . A large flock of Canada geese grazed in the shelter of the dunes. One bar-headed goose was with them, an 'escapee' from a collection.

Over on the old saltmarsh skylarks chirruped. A small flock of green-finches rose and resettled. Now we had reached the sea. The wind was blowing the waves into white-maned horses. Along the shoreline scooted eight pearly-grey and white sanderlings. A purple sandpiper flew by. We sea-watched from the shelter of the remains of past coastal defences. Concrete blocks made excellent rests for telescopes.

Ten scoters – sea ducks – bobbed offshore. Eight cormorants headed steadily west. Six 'bonxies' passed by . . . and a dark-phase arctic skua . . . and a 'comic' tern. Stormy weather brings in exciting birds for the seawatcher.

The tide was advancing. It crept closer and closer. At last it was splashing over our feet and we were forced to retreat. We walked back slowly along the sea wall, listening to the calling of redshanks. The elegant black tern was still skimming and dipping, a rhythmical rise and fall: perhaps the biggest treat of the day – in a day full of treats.

O·C·T·O·B·E·R

Honey Fungus Still for Tea

Charnwood Forest, Leicestershire

When birdwatching in October, it is nice to have an expert on fungi in the group and to end the day with a gourmet fry-up. 'Another slice of parasol?' 'Who's for a morsel of shaggy inkcap?' 'A soupçon of cep?'

We met at the edge of Charnwood Forest on a mild damp morning in a privately owned wood set amid outcrops of some of the oldest rock in the British Isles. I had come prepared with a basket for edible trophies, 'food for free'. But this time, it soon became obvious, our mycologist (fungi-expert) was no mycophagist (fungi-eater). 'Is this good to eat?' I asked eagerly, the first few times we stopped beside a munchy-looking mushroom/toadstool. 'Well, I wouldn't want to chance it,' 'Not one I'd fancy.' 'Bit dicey,' came the laconic replies.

Tom was interested in shape, texture, colour, smell – and putting a *name* (and Latin at that) to each species. The possibility of eating our finds came well down the list. It would be scrambled egg for tea again, not mushrooms, it seemed.

The blue flash of a jay's wing-feathers . . . and the bird flew out with a screech; we had disturbed its feasting upon acorns, abundant on the mature oaks which grew in the wood. Beneath one oak grew an indented, funnel-shaped brown toadstool. Our expert sniffed.

'*Lactarius quietus*,' he pronounced. 'Oily milkcap,' he translated for us novices. He broke off a piece of the cap and drops of a milky juice oozed from the flesh. 'All milkcaps exude a milky juice. This one smells of bedbugs, don't you think.' He passed the oily milkcap round for us to smell and to judge for ourselves. But no one present would admit to knowledge of bedbug odour. As well as 'oily milkcap', the species is known as 'oak milkcap' and 'mild milkcap' – which explains why it is so necessary to persevere with Latin nomenclature. Besides, he added, many species have no common English name.

Smell, we learned, is an important clue to identification. During the next few hours we sniffed at a *Russula fragilis* and agreed, 'apple'; at the false deathcap (*Amanita citrina*) 'raw potatoes'; at *Mycena inclinata*, 'soap'; at the common puffball (*Lycoperdon perlatum*), 'radish'.

But the most unforgettable and revolting odour of the day came from the stinkhorns (*Phallus impudicus*) which smell of rotting flesh and thus attract flies which feed on the slimy green spore-containing jelly on the bell-shaped head of the thick white stem.

Sometimes we identified by feel. The butter cap (*Collybia butyracea*) was greasy to the touch, as if smeared with butter. The *Boletus* toadstools were spongy-textured. The toothed edges of the gills of *Russula fragilis* could be felt with our fingers, but carefully, for *Russula fragilis* is, indeed, fragile. Birch polypore (*Polyporus betulinus*) feels smooth, like fine leather. It grows only on silver birch trees and looks like a fat kidney-shaped cushion.

We smelt, we felt – and we looked. 'Look for veil-remnants, a good identity-aid.' Some toadstools first appear as small knobs with a thin protective tissue. Moisture is absorbed, the toadstool expands and tears the tissue 'veil'. We found a parasol (*Lepiota procera*) at the wood's edge, its cap veil flaked and its stalk with a frilly veil-collar. The scarlet cap of fly agaric (*Amanita muscaria*) – beloved by illustrators of children's books – is white-spotted with such veil remnants. More veil skirted its stalk. No gnome on top – but a frog posed rather nicely on an old tree stump from which grew large clusters of the poisonous sulphur tuft.

We looked at, without touching, the even more poisonous false death cap and noted its veil-remnant 'sock', baggy round the base of the stem. Never touch a toadstool with a bulbous bottom, we were warned.

Colour and shape identified for us shaggy ink cap, false chanterelle, penny bun, the blusher – our list grew long.

Millions of spores are produced by the fruiting bodies of fungi. A spore which survives and settles sends out tiny threads (hyphae) which feed by releasing enzymes to break down the living or dead host material into simple minerals, a form which it can absorb. The tangled mass of hyphae spreads and matures and, when conditions are right – autumnal rainfall, damp nights after warm summer days – it produces the fruiting bodies (mushrooms, toadstools) which swell and push their way above ground.

Most spores are simply released and blown away by the wind. Puffballs wait for the drip of rain on their hollow skins to act as spore releasers. We found a puddle and dripped mock raindrops – and watched the spores puff out. But the thick scaly skin of the earthball cracks as it dries, to let its spores escape. From out of a log of wood branched weird candlesnuff (*Xylaria hypoxylon*) with a black base and white, powdery, snuffed-out 'wick'. Into my basket it

Fly agaric

Honey fungus

'Basket of inedible trophies.'

went; and so did *Helvella crispa* with fluted, wrinkled stem and saddle-shaped cap. By now the basket was almost full of fascinating – if inedible – trophies which would look attractive on my mantelpiece for a day or two.

Then we discovered a violet-mauve wood blewit (*Tricholoma nudum*). Even our leader shared the enthusiasm for this exciting culinary find. Wood blewits are delicious. We found another. 'We'll give them to our host,' we agreed.

The owner of the wood looked pleased at the gift – but not so pleased when we pointed out a spread of honey fungus (*Armillaria mellea*) on the edge of his garden. This parasite, great destroyer of trees and shrubs, sends out 'bootlace' threads (which glow phosphorescently at night) to devour the living wood.

'Honey fungus is edible if cooked, isn't it,' I asked, suddenly remembering.

'Help yourself,' said our host eagerly, 'yes, it's quite good fried in butter.' So we had a fungi fry-up – and not scrambled eggs – for tea after all.

Deer Country
Exmoor

I was back again, at a Field Studies Council centre. This time, staying at Nettlecombe Court, the Leonard Wills Field Centre, close to the edge of Exmoor National Park. I had come for the birds of the Westcountry – and I wanted to see red deer, Britain's largest land mammal.

It is quite possible for a stranger to visit the vast wild lonely stretch of Exmoor, part Devon, part Somerset – and not see one of its reputed thousand red deer. Only a native, a life-long observer of this shy, secretive animal who knows its favourite haunts, can guarantee sightings.

As one would expect, the Field Studies Council has found such a man. Dick Lloyd was born inside the National Park boundaries and works as manager on a big Exmoor farm. I wanted to learn all I could from him of the moor and its wildlife.

In our wellies and dark rustle-proof clothing, the group of us drove first to Dulverton to follow the winding River Barle through its wooded valley. The leaves on the trees were changing now from green to the rich russet-reds and yellow ochres of autumn. The bracken was already turned to brown: bronze in the glinting sunlight.

Then we were up on the heather-purpled moorland. Meadow pipits rose in a flock and swirled and settled. Dick's sharp eyes quickly detected the day's first red deer. It was October, the season of the rut, when stags round up their harems and defend them aggressively with much scrapping and roaring. Through binoculars we could see four hinds now, browsing on the fresh green leaves of the heather which were already shooting up from beneath the tough

Nettlecombe Court

grey branches of the old. One hind had with her a calf. It would have been born back in June, its red coat dappled with creamy spots, a charmer. But spots and dappling had long vanished.

'It's a male,' said Dick, 'with a shorter, thicker neck. There is somehow a *tougher* look about him, even at this age, an uprightness in his carriage. He is still young enough to suckle but he'll soon be independent – although he'll follow on behind his mother for some weeks yet.'

The hinds were vari-coloured, their coats glossy after the good feeding of the summer months. Fox-red, sandy, chestnut; the diversity surprised us. But all had cream-coloured rumps. Winter coats, which had already begun to grow, would be greyer in tone.

A buzzard flew low with prey in its talons. It landed in the bracken and vanished out of sight. Skylarks chirruped . . . flocking lapwing . . . and a lone snipe whirred up and zig-zagged across our path.

Photographers wanted to get close to the deer, to stalk with cameras. Dick drove us to the Horner Valley, between Dunkery and the sea ('the real Exmoor,' said Dick). He halted the mini-bus alongside a steep gully. Five hundred yards away grazed more deer. We pinpointed their position: stunted hawthorn tree, a blaze of yellow gorse, two large boulders. Dick Lloyd led at a fast pace along the gully – out of sight and downwind of our quarry.

Negotiating slippery stones, a stream crossing, squelchy mud and scratchy bracken he led us to the spot below the hawthorn tree. We started to crawl up the slope to the top, keeping heads low. At a signal from Dick, we silently rose to our feet, focussed cameras – and clicked. Three beautiful slender-necked hinds looked our way with dark, long-lashed eyes. A majestic stag, with a shaggy grey mane and a splendid head of antlers ('All his rights, and three a-top both sides,' said Dick) stood a little apart on guard, silhouetted against blue sky.

Dick cupped his hands and roared a great throaty roar, a fine imitation of the 'belling' of a stag in the rut. The animal turned to gaze – we clicked! It was a thrilling moment.

'If we were just a bit nearer, we would smell him. A stag's scent is heavy and rank at this time.'

For a few short weeks only the rut (mating season) lasts. Stags, uninterested for the rest of the year, keep close watch on their 'girls' – only to be challenged time and time again by later arrivals. Wandering bachelors keep stags with harems in a constant state of tension, said Dick.

We crept away. And walked next across farmland, past high beech hedges and fields where sheep cropped the grass. Exmoor ponies, with mealy pale-coloured noses, moved away at our approach. In a muddy patch we saw tracks which, said our leader, were not those of a sheep.

'Deer prints' said Dick. 'The shape is less square, the slots narrow and more pointed, the heels rounded. This one is two inches across – there's the dew claw imprint; if the dew claws show, you know you are on to a *heavy* stag.'

He drew his finger through the mud and compared the two impressions. 'Made in the last twelve hours,' he decided.

It wasn't a 'heavy' stag that we saw shortly afterwards, but a young one – 'all his rights and nothing 'a-top'. Dick, of course, had his glasses on him first; I found it well nigh impossible to pick out the vari-coloured beasts with the naked eye, so perfectly did they blend with their background.

'Probably in his fifth year – but statements concerning age must always be made with caution,' we were warned.

Each stag is an individual and there is considerable variation between heads – as the pairs of antlers are termed. Splendid examples are seen on Exmoor (Dick was to show us some 'trophies' later) for the living is good and quality depends on available food.

In his second year, a male is known as a 'pricket' and he bears two knobs which grow from the permanent stumps of bone ('pedicles') on the skull between the ears. In the following years, 'brow', 'bay' and 'tray' points ('tines') are usually added to the 'beam'. Then a stag is said to have 'all his rights'. The heads of six, seven, eight and nine-year-olds grow ever more magnificent as points are added a-top. After ten years, heads start to 'go back' and the antlers of an old stag are short and warped. 'Velvet', the overlying furry skin, is shed as the summer passes. Blood-filled antlers are transformed into hard, insensitive weapons with which to fight.

The young stag below us now on the edge of a small copse was on guard. His harem of six pretty hinds peacefully chewed the cud, enjoying the sun's warmth. Unless he remained ever watchful, a rival could oust him – often after a fight featuring much hefty pushing and a great clashing of antlers. Rutting goes on into November and sometimes the racket of the 'belling' continues all night, an eerie sound.

Another broad-winged buzzard soared above us as we stood on the great watershed called The Chains, a desolate grassy plain broken by many streams which drop swiftly down precipitous slopes. The northern streams (or 'waters') find their way to the sea at Lynmouth. The southern waters are tributaries of the Barle. We were high enough to see something of the wild Exmoor coastline, a long stretch of spectacular cliff and the cleft which is Porlock Bay. We could see across to the island of Lundy. The wind blew chill from the sea and we remembered – we were in Doone country. ('And every woman clutched her child and every man turned pale at the very name of Doone.')

Later, in the shelter of a wood, Dick told us that woodland is the natural habitat of red deer. Stags, as they move through the trees, must lift their heads high so that antlers lie back on either side of the body and do not impede progress. Even in the depth of winter a variety of food is available in woodland: hips and haws, acorns, rowan berries, elder, bramble, ivy, young tree shoots, fungi and moss – deer will eat almost any vegetation.

Unfortunately, added Dick, food preferences include farm crops. They lie in, and roll about on, growing cereal. They nibble at oats. They uproot turnips and swedes, discarding each after just one bite. And they break down fences and damage hedges – to the consternation of farmers. Which is why deer numbers need to be controlled.

It was near Dunkery Beacon, Exmoor's highest point, that we watched high drama as a usurper 'stole' a hind and calf from a fellow stag's harem and an exciting chase followed over heather and bracken for several hundred yards. Then the 'master' stag braked, remembered the rest of his now unguarded hinds – still grazing unconcernedly – decided to cut his losses and trotted back to the knoll, roaring his fury.

A curlew flew over, clear-piping, and a twittering pack of golden plover flashed white and gold in the glare of the setting sun as the birds circled and banked.

That night we talked over, in the field centre's bar, the amazing sights we had seen that day. The graceful leap of a hind over a high wire fence; the stag party of youngsters trotting though the bracken in follow-my-leader fashion; the bare polished branches of a stag's withy bush rubbing post; the snorting bark of the hind; the 'twelve-pointer' we had stalked.

Red deer, running wild, add immeasurably – we all agreed – to the beauty and interest of the magnificent Devon/ Somerset border country known as Exmoor.

Superbird

Cley-next-the-Sea, Norfolk

We were slogging our way along the deeply shelving ridge of shingle between Cley and Salthouse on the Norfolk coast when we found it, the tiny sad corpse of a goldcrest.

'There's one small migrant that didn't quite make it,' said my companion. Ironically it had survived the bleak crossing of the North Sea and reached the coastline, only to succumb, exhausted.

Birds were still on the move, this October day, arriving from the continent to winter, or to pass through to seek a surety of food and warmth in hospitable regions further south. A few minutes ago we had surprised snow buntings.

The flock rose suddenly into the air and moved along the ridge, individuals 'leap-frog-flying', overtaking in turn, for short distances, snowflake-wings spread. They drifted along the beach, to resettle gently. Once grounded, and with wings closed, their brown, buff, black and ochre patterning merges into the mottled shingle surround.

Ravenous after their long journey – snow buntings breed in Greenland and Scandinavia – they searched for food on the shingle of the ridge and on the saltmarsh below. Flowers were dead, or fading fast, but a few specimens still brightened with petal colour, even in October, the sombre pebbles and saltmarsh mud: yellow-horned poppies, sea campion, sea bindweed and sea holly. Late flowering, late fruiting plants offering seed sustenance to passage and wintering shoreline birds.

We checked the legs of the tiny fragile goldcrest corpse. No numbered ring to tell us where it came from, but there might have been. Authorised ringers are busy in many countries, linked by the EURING Scheme.

But numbered rings, coloured rings, wing tags, plumage dyes, and all the other simple devices used to track birds on migration in past years, are being rapidly supplanted by new technological aids. Advances in knowledge have increased accordingly.

Flight paths can be mapped by light aircraft equipped with searchlights – for most birds migrate at night in large scale wide front movements. Individual birds are fitted with transmitters which send back signals. Flocks show up on radar screens, and some birdwatching groups now own refined radar tracking systems. Calls made in flight can be interpreted by conversion to sonograms on oscilloscope screens. Frequency of wingbeats are scientifically 'read' to give species identification.

In the last few years controlled experiments suggest that birds may well possess a truly remarkable range of skills. Hypotheses put forward thirty years ago – and scoffed at – are being tested, with surprising results.

How important an aid is sight? A pigeon, fitted with frosted glass contact lenses which impede vision, can still fly, with little difficulty, straight back home. So landmark recognition, of mountains, rivers, coastlines, peninsulas, is not the vital navigational aid it was once thought. Does the pigeon use the earth's magnetic field? If a small magnet bar is attached to the bird to cause confusion in its magnetic field readings, it will still find its way home on a sunny day. On an overcast day, it is puzzled and disorientated. It seems to derive important directional information from the earth's magnetic field when need – poor visibility – dictates.

Other experiments suggest that birds are sensitive to both ultra-violet light and to polarised light. Their sense of smell is acute. They can detect infra-sounds, such as wind and sea, over long distances. They are able, it seems, to make use of reliable winds and are sufficiently resilient to adapt to freak fluctuations. It is likely they are capable of responding to the irregular variations of the earth's gravity and, by detecting changes in barometric pressure, able to forecast weather fronts.

Any, or all, of these options may well be called upon as back-up cues, each with its own value in the particular circumstance, when basic celestial cues – position of sun, or moon and stars – are absent.

Research seems to confirm that a bird possesses the incredible ability to gauge compass directions by the star map at night and the sun by day with the help of its own 'internal clock'. Migrants appear able to forecast the weather in advance and to set out in optimum conditions: clear skies and favourable following winds. Some species even use a different migratory route in spring and autumn; to make use of seasonal winds?

All this does not mean that birds *never* get lost. As we neared the end of that Norfolk shingle ridge we were told by other birdwatchers, 'Pallas' leaf-warbler at Holkham.'

We stood under the pine trees of Holkham until the sun began to set. Pallas' leaf-warbler is a foliage gleaner. It habitually hovers to pick food off leaves. I directed my binoculars at a shiver of leaves in the undergrowth. But the shiver-causer was a mundane blue tit and could not possibly be mistaken for that poor wee gone-astray (feather-brained? flighty?) Asiatic waif, so far to the west of its regular route.

Had its compass-reading let it down? Was it not up to scratch on its knowledge of the earth's magnetic field? Had it forgotten to compensate for 'drift'? Or had its internal clock stopped? Its 'barometer', perhaps, did not warn of the approach of an anticyclone with treacherous easterly flow?

The tiny foliage-gleaner did not appear. It was probably a young bird, still learning all those navigational skills and, sadly, unlikely to survive. But ringing recoveries are proof that occasional birds can set themselves to rights after serious straying.

So I like to think our Pallas' warbler had already reset its 'altimeter', read its 'sextant', turned its back on the dying rays of the sun to the west, looked up at the first twinkling star, listened to far-away infra-sounds – and flown neatly over our heads on its migratory way.

Ruddy duck

Stifftails

Blithfield Reservoir, Rugeley, Staffordshire

'Ruddy duck!' exclaimed my companion. I glanced at her askance. It was not like her to swear. 'Escaped from Slimbridge in the fifties. Member of the stifftail tribe. Took to breeding in the wild. Increased in number at rate of 25 per cent a year. Admitted to the British List of Breeding Birds in 1971.'

'Oh, *ruddy* duck,' I said, understanding.

We were at Blithfield Reservoir. We had left our cars on the causeway, watched the sailing boats to the south for a while and then, armed with permits issued by the West Midlands Bird Club, we set about exploring the considerable expanse of water to the north.

Six snipe in the reedbeds waited hidden until we were close and then towered up, out and over the reservoir, to zigzag their way circuitously back into the reeds. Kingfishers, two of them, swift-darted through willows allowing tantalising glimpses of stunning electric-blue shot-silk plumage. In a conifer plantation goldcrests fleetingly materialised and jays showed bright blue wing flashes against the needle-darkness.

We reached a copse of broad-leaved trees. A female sparrowhawk swerved out and soared high on rounded wings to escape the mobbing of carrion crows. Twenty agile siskins in the branches of alder trees picked out seeds from the tiny alder cones. Their yellow wing-bars caught the light. A single oak tree with leaves an autumnal mix of colours – dark green, black, brown and yellow ochre – sheltered two nuthatches, two lesser spotted woodpeckers, one treecreeper and one goldcrest. And parties of mixed tits showed blue against the sombre browns of a late autumn hedge.

So there was a richness of sightings in a variety of habitats. But it was the wildfowl on the water that we had really come to see. Blithfield attracts good numbers. Over 3,000 wildfowl of thirteen different species winter on its 800 acres. Ducks, geese and swans, searching for shelter, seclusion and sustenance, arrive each year. They come from as far away as Siberia, Greenland, Iceland and Scandinavia, driven south by howling arctic winds and icy blizzards.

Many wetlands have shrunk, or disappeared altogether in Britain. New lowland reservoirs built over the last forty years are welcomed by birds as a safe substitute refuge. Blithfield is one of them.

The construction of Blithfield began in 1952. At the first trickle of water, wildfowl began to fly in. First the dabblers: mallard, gadwall, pintail, wigeon, shoveler and teal – and mute and Bewick swans. They paddled in the shallows of flooding farmland, enjoying abundant nutrient-rich food.

Then, as the water deepened and aquatic invertebrates multiplied, the diving ducks arrived: tufted, goldeneye, pochard and goosander. Only Abberton Reservoir in Essex and Rutland Water in Leicestershire can boast larger numbers.

On this Sunday in November Canada geese grazed in surrounding fields. Sixty wigeon fed in a close compact flock at the water's edge. On the rippling waves of the man-made lake floated tufted duck, goldeneye, teal, mallard, shoveler and great crested grebe. We settled on the grass, binoculars handy, to picnic with thermos flasks of steaming coffee and boxes of sandwiches. It was then we saw the first small party of ruddy ducks.

They bobbed jauntily, dived with a smooth sleek action – and bobbed up again: stiff rudder-tails, short dumpy bodies, prominent bills.

More small flotillas came into view. We counted a total of two hundred ruddy ducks. The bright feathers of the drakes had moulted and they were in winter plumage. Gone was the chestnut ruddiness, the cobalt blue of the bill,

Goldcrest

the startling whiteness of the large cheek patches which make ruddy ducks such attractive little birds in summer. Winter plumage is subdued, male and female almost become look-alikes – separated only by the cheek patch, black-speckled now, of the drake.

The ruddy duck is not a native bird. In 1948 three pairs were imported from North America by the Wildfowl Trust. At Slimbridge they bred happily. A few broods escaped notice and the ducklings, which remain in the nest for only a few hours after hatching, went unpinioned. Between 1956 and 1963 a number of full-winged birds flew from the Trust grounds.

In 1960 an escapee pair raised a family at Chew Valley Reservoir in the county of Avon. Now many small pools and meres throughout the Midlands, the northwest, the Welsh border counties and beyond, hold pairs of ruddy ducks in summer time. They build small floating platform nests, anchor them to reeds, and lay eggs which hatch in June and July.

In spite of the fact that their cousins back home in North America migrate to the sunspots of California and Florida in autumn, our ruddy duck settlers manage to survive British winters. It is agreed that they are hardy, successful – and here to stay and are now adopted officially as 'British Breeding Birds'.

At the end of summer, they vacate their secret breeding pools and congregate on certain favourite reservoirs: Blithfield, Blagdon, Chew Valley, Belvide and Swithland. Only if the water freezes over will they disperse and fly elsewhere in search of better conditions.

So what is so special about Blithfield and Belvide in Staffordshire, Chew Valley and Blagdon in Avon and Swithland Reservoir in Leicestershire? The water in these reservoirs is shallow enough for a small duck to reach without difficulty the food it needs from the muddy ooze at the bottom; boats are banned from a large area; and the natural reedy margins, spits and bays provide shelter.

Ruddy ducks are the only representative of the stifftail tribe to be found wild in Britain, but they are, of course, an introduced species, properly native to North America. The only *true* European stifftail is the white-headed duck – and it can be seen in the Slimbridge collection.

The white-headed duck is short-necked and dumpy. The drake's white head is capped with a black crown; his bill, broad and swollen at the base, is bright blue; his breast and back are chestnut-red and speckled. He moves smoothly as if by clockwork, head high and tail usually flat on the water – except during courtship, when it's raised perkily. He woos his mate with a 'tickering purr' call.

But these odd and attractive little stifftails have disappeared from several European countries. The Wildfowl Trust's programme of captive-breeding has made possible, in recent years, its return to Hungary. British Airways (slogan: 'Assisting Nature Conservation') is generous with its sponsorship and gave VIP treatment to batches of eggs. Flown in a specially constructed incubator, the enterprise received much media attention. The eggs hatched, the ducks were released into an area of sandy steppes and shallow lakes in the

Kiskunsag National Park – and Hungary now has back its stifftails.

And, at Blithfield today, we were watching another stifftail, the ruddy duck. We finished our picnic and continued on our way to the far side of the reservoir. With Fred in the lead, we negotiated a precarious log bridge and squelched in our wellies through soggy mud alongside the River Blythe. As the light began to fade, we followed the tortuous path back through woodland.

A tawny owl panicked and fled. Thousands of gulls, lesser black-backed and black-headed, flew in to roost on the water for the night. Fourteen splendid goosanders floated beneath the causeway, their breasts glowing pink in the low rays of the setting sun.

But our last sighting as we reached the cars was of a straggly line of ruddy duck stifftails, buoyantly afloat, dark silhouettes in a November dusk.

Early Winter Birds
Betws-y-coed, North Wales

I woke early. Through my bedroom window I could see thousands of starlings streaming across the red ball of the rising sun. Flocks had left their night time roosts and were heading for daytime feeding grounds.

The view, with its panorama of mountains, foretold of the winter to come. Bracken on the wooded slopes had faded to brown. Autumnal-tinted leaves still clung precariously to branches. The first strong gale would bare the trees to skeletons.

I joined the others for an early breakfast. Then, from the Drapers' Field Centre, we walked across the fields towards the River Conwy to look for birds. Betws-y-coed ('sanctuary in the wood') stands at the junction of the three rivers, Conwy, Llugwy and Lledr. As the sun warmed the earth, so a mist rose and hung low over the valley.

A voluminous dark yew tree stood close to a stone wall. Redwings, winter visitors from Scandinavia, were enjoying the sticky pink yew berries; they flew in and out, with soft, 'seep, seep' calls, and 'choop, choops', showing off chestnut flanks and creamy eye-stripes. The seeds of the yew berries are poisonous; the birds eat the flesh and the seed passes harmlessly through the gut.

From a tall conifer a nuthatch piped its single note call, 'Pi-pi-pi-pi.' The little bird moved in jerks, up and down and sideways, then clung, head downward, to the trunk giving us a splendid view of its delicate blue and apricot colours and sleek outline.

A large black corvid flew across. A raven, I wondered? It slowed, flipped right over, flipped . . . flipped again, fell through the air, righted itself and flew off in the direction of the mountains, with a rich deep 'Kronk, kronk, kronk.' Yes, a raven! Showing off its acrobatics.

We were on an 'early winter birds' weekend course, led by John Hall. He told us that few birds stay in the mountains in winter. Conditions are too hard. They come down to the valleys for shelter and food, moving southwards or westwards if the weather worsens. The hardy crows and ravens are the exceptions for they can be found in the tops all the year round. Skylarks, meadow pipits, golden plovers, grey wagtails, dippers vacate the heights. Ring ouzels and wheatears emigrate from Britain altogether.

Berries, fruiting abundantly in the lowlands, are a mainstay for many birds. Hedgerows continue well-berried through many of the crucial months, patched dark red with haws, bright red with hips, purple-black with elder-berries. Today the last of the blackberries hung plump and juicy, a few orange berries remained in depleted rowan tree larders, scarlet holly berries and white snow-berries were on offer – but scarcely touched as yet. Ivy berries looked green and inedible; they ripen in spring, a last source of berry-food for hungry thrushes.

Fallen leaves from oak and hawthorn crunched underfoot. We reached the river. A silver salmon leapt in the splashing foaming torrent. Six mallards flew over and we picked out the curly tails of the drakes. On the edge of a shingle bank a grey wagtail quivered and darted after flies – an insectivorous bird which cannot adapt to a vegetarian life style and so has a hard time of it in a severe winter.

Next we saw a dipper. It zipped downstream and landed, to bob for us on a ledge beneath a small bridge. Then it blinked its white eyelids and whirred off and out of sight.

Acorns littered our path, food for jays and crows which cache the nuts for future eating in secret holes in the ground. Suddenly a large brown bird flew fast and low across a gap in the hedge opposite in pursuit of a squawking blackbird. It was a female sparrowhawk, but we were not to see the end of the chase; maybe the blackbird escaped. The secret weapons of a sparrowhawk are surprise attack and its agility. Typically it flicks through trees and along hedgerows after small birds.

We left the river bank to follow the path back across the fields. Black-headed gulls streamed past, more birds on their way to the sea. White flashes on the leading edges of wings identified them. The chocolate brown caps of summer had dwindled to small brown spots.

We heard a moorhen's grating squeak and saw its hasty sidle into the shelter of reeds. A wren's loud tick warned of our coming. Lapwings took off with much commotion and tumbled and swooped with floppy wings. A jackdaw watched our progress from the dead branch of a tree with glass-bright beady eyes. Rooks – resembling 'badly stuffed crows' – bald patches around beaks, raggedy 'trousers', searched for wire-worms in the fields.

We arrived back at the Field Centre, collected our packed lunches, and the

Hawthorn berries

mini-bus drove us down-river to where it widened – the top of the estuary. We looked across the broad expanse of water. On the far bank a dozen waders dozed, proving a puzzle at first for the colour of legs was hidden by the long grass and bills were tucked under wings. We flicked through our field guides, considering possibilities. Then a loud 'Tyuuu, tyuuu, tyuuu,' solved the mystery. There is no mistaking the redshank's warning call. And there! the red legs and bill of one wide awake, wing-stretching wader.

A large heavy all-black bird flew past low over the water, long wings beating with slow powerful strokes. Cormorant or shag? Probably cormorant, we decided. It was rather far up river for the sea-loving shag.

In an alder tree one lone yellow and green siskin busily probed into cones for seeds. A boat chugged past, its vigorous wash disturbing the reedbeds. Out flew five snipe. Up they towered with jinking flight – as if they'd evolved flight tactics to avoid the guns of sportsmen blazing away at them!

'Crek, crek,' the snipe called as they circled up and over the river, then jinked crazily back to resettle in the reeds. For one of our group it was the first 'wisp' ever and the excitement was almost too much for her. 'I could see their long beaks *with my naked eyes!*' she gasped.

We thought we were in for more excitement as we listened to the description given to us of a strange 'bird' advancing in midstream – as seen through the binoculars of another member of the group. Then – 'Oh, but it's a *woodwink*,' he exclaimed as a curiously shaped log floated by – and he realised he'd been hoodwinked!

Mid-morning: coffee time. As we unscrewed our flasks we realised that the weekend had scarcely begun, and yet already we had seen a number of memorable birds. With berries on the bushes, wintering waders, and migrants from the mountains, a Welsh valley in early winter is a good place to be.

Waiting for the Tide

Menai Straits, North Wales

We stood behind a row of wooden groynes and waited for the tide to push the birds up towards us. We were on an estuary, the mouth of the River Ogwen. Behind us were the mountains. On the far bank stood Penrhyn Castle. In front of us lay the Lavan Sands, a vast stretch of mudflats which, in two hours time, would be covered by the sea.

In spite of the fact that bad weather had been forecast, the sky was blue and the sea tranquil. Gales at this time of the year can blow in some surprising birds but, as we rested our arms on those convenient wooden groyne posts to peer through our binoculars and telescopes, we could feel the thin rays of the sun on our backs and were quite content to make do with 'regulars'.

'The two hours before high tide and the two hours after are the best times,' said John, 'otherwise the birds are so far away that eyes just pop out of sockets.'

My binoculars focussed on a small brown wader at the water's edge. Its black and white eye mask and broad black collar identified it as a ringed plover. (The *little* ringed plover is smaller, with a white line running round its crown and a prominent yellow eye ring.)

Redshanks on the far shore fed busily. Amongst them was a stranger. 'In front of the pipe coming out of the stone wall, to the left a bit, near where the three oystercatchers are standing,' we were directed. But it is not always easy to locate a bird through binoculars at such a distance. 'Look with eyes first, find the bird and remain focussed keeping your head still,' advised John, 'then, carefully, raise your binocs.'

Flocks of winter waders often contain a solitary bird of a different species. The odd-one-out this time was larger than its redshank neighbours, and darker-plumaged with dark legs. We concentrated on the bill which appeared, at first sight, to be straight. It was not extremely long and deeply curved like the curlew's bill; or uptilted slightly, like the godwit's. The mystery bird changed position. Now we had a cleaner view of its profile. The bill curved downwards at the tip. And by this time someone had it in his 'scope.

'Dark crown with central stripe; white eye-stripe,' We were looking at a whimbrel. (Curlews = streaky heads; whimbrels = striped heads.) Late passage migrant? Perhaps. Whimbrels don't usually winter in Britain.

Britain is a 'staging post' on the East Atlantic fly-way. Millions of birds fly through each spring and autumn, using estuaries as refuelling stops. But it was now early winter. We expected to see the winter visitors which exploit the rich feeding grounds of the Menai Straits between November and March.

The mouth of a river provides plentiful food. Organic remains, both animal and vegetable, are washed down by the stream or brought in with the tide and these attract vast numbers of estuarine invertebrates.

The boulder on which a pale-bellied young cormorant had been standing was now under water. And the tide was bringing in ducks and grebes. A pair of beautiful pintail preened, perhaps relishing the feel of freshwater brought down by the river. A scattering of great crested grebes rode the waves. The haunting call of wigeon, a high-pitched 'wheeyoo, wheeyoo' carried across the bay above the pipe of redshank, clamour of gulls and 'kleep, kleep' whistle of oystercatcher.

'Red-breasted merganser steaming up the channel.'

A whole flotilla of the fish-eating sawbills had appeared. They, too, began to preen. The drake merganser is striking with his wispy punk headcrest, large white wing patches, thin red bill, dark head and white collar. 'The ragged head shape is the give-away.'

There must have been around sixty pairs buoyantly afloat in the estuary. The Lavan Sands (Traeth Lafan) is an important gathering site for red-breasted mergansers, birds which typically winter in coastal waters. The other large British sawbill, the goosander, prefers lakes and reservoirs.

John hoped that we would remember the 'ragged head' shape of the merganser. His aim was to make each one of us an *independent* birdwatcher. Beginners tend to rely for too long on other people's identifications. 'Work it out for yourself,' he said.

Another excitement. Someone had sighted a goldeneye. Its oddly peaked headshape gives it away. No white blob on the dark cheek – so it was a female. With a neat little spring – up and under – it disappeared from view, to reappear thirty yards away.

But the goldeneye was quickly forgotten when the red-throated diver appeared offshore, an uncommon happening on the north coast of Wales. The bird came right into the bay and stationed itself close to a rock. The red on the throat had vanished in the post-breeding moult. But it was unmistakeably a diver, a big, powerful, reptilian-looking bird; pale-fringed with grey/brown flecking on the neck, a grey back spotted with white and a beak which turned up slightly at the tip.

It swam briefly, surging through the water with head and neck lowered flat, hunching its back: a sea monster. Then it reared up out of the water, showing a long white belly, and continued its vigorous preening.

The tide was nearly high now. Waders, finding their feeding area flooded, became restless. They took to the air. We were treated to fly-pasts of dunlin, showing off their synchronised 'all together now' swirling turns before they settled to roost. Lapwing and curlew and black-headed gulls headed for inland fields where they would rest and wait patiently for the tide to turn. Oystercatchers, with their new white winter collars, hunched together on a shingle spit roost, facing into the wind, balanced on one leg, red bills tucked into scapulars, feathers fluffed, pink eyes glowing.

The water was lapping at the wooden groynes which had served us so well. Everything had stopped for the high tide. Birds ceased their constant search for food. It was snooze time. The idea appealed. We retreated to a suitable loafing site, stretched stiff limbs – and joined the snoozing throng.

Earlier that day we had visited two other key points on the Menai Straits. We crept up on a small flock of ringed plovers foraging on a black slate beach. Seven we counted, then looked again. There was a turnstone too, we had nearly missed it, its bright tortoiseshell plumage changed to the grey of winter and its drabness merging into the dark slate background. It flew a short way, showing off the zigzag pattern on its wings. The turnstone was the 'odd one out' amongst the ringed plovers.

A flock of finches can hide a brambling; look for the brambling's white rump. Check a fly-past of gulls; is every wing black-tipped? An all-white gull may be a rare *little* gull. If a flight of redshanks comes into view, check that the trailing edge of each wing is gleaming white: there may be a whimbrel, or a paler, longer-legged spotted redshank, or a heavy grey plover with black under the wing – in among the red-legged waders.

Next, a bleak saltmarsh. Starlings smoked across the sky, swirled, and landed in sea purslane. Pied wagtails strutted alongside narrow channels and darted after flies. A heron peered with long, upstretched snaky neck. Skylarks and linnets, in roller-coaster flight, seed-searched, making throaty – or twittering – contact calls.

Then we had driven to the Lavan Sands to wait for high tide to push the birds up to us.

We roused ourselves. The tide had turned and was on the retreat. Birds were flying back from the fields. We drove to a cliff top which overlooked a muddy bay. Curlew, redshank, ringed plover, dunlin and oystercatcher – congregated in species groups – squidged over the exposed and glistening wet mud.

In the shallow water two hundred of the goose-like conspicuous shelducks swooshed red bills from side to side. Further out, they up-ended in the deeper water and, on the shore itself, scooped and sifted mud. Shelduck had only recently returned from their annual moult migration on the mudflats of the Wadden Sea. Exceptionally for ducks, the females accompany the males, leaving ducklings in crèches in the care of a few stay-at-home adults. Ducks and drakes are rendered flightless for several weeks. Again exceptionally, the plumage of both sexes is very similar, and the eclipse plumage only differs slightly.

Shelduck feed on tiny laver spire shells present in vast numbers on mudflats. The shells are so tiny (only 4mm long) that the ducks must consume them in large quantities. By using different feeding methods – scything, upending, dabbling – they can feed through most hours of the clock if necessary. The laver shells float in rafts on the surface of the water, consuming algae. They are washed in with the tide and sink down on to the newly exposed mud, giving it a gritty look. After feeding on organic material for a while, they burrow into the mud and await the next tide, to attach themselves, upside down, to the surface film of the water. The cycle begins again, and shelduck adapt their feeding methods accordingly. But what were all the *waders* feeding on?

It was cold on the exposed cliff face, the weather had deteriorated. Scuds of rain hit us. The beginner birdwatchers were wishing they had put on a few more layers. Their ungloved fingers froze as they tried to hold binoculars steady. We took pity on them and drove down into Bangor. In the harbour, above a sewage outlet pipe, hundreds of gulls were squabbling and gorging. On the mud, redshanks probed.

John got out spades and buckets from the back of the mini-bus. 'Now to find out what waders feed on.' He squelched over the pongy mud. The bravest of us followed after. Redshanks panicked and fled, piping shrilly, 'Tyuuuuu, tyuuuuu.' The mud smelt terrible: bad eggs. I got stuck. My foot was held down by clogging mud. I chopped at it with the spade I was carrying. Out came my welly-booted leg with a loud squelch. A hefty pull at the other leg, which had gradually been sinking lower all the while, freed me. I stopped being an intrepid explorer and plodged back to safety.

John returned with samples which we emptied into sieves. First a shrimpy thing wriggled into view, a tiny burrow-living amphipod. With its long antennae it reaches up and scrapes organic debris off the surrounding surface, drawing it back into its hole to eat in safety. Comparative safety, that is, for if a redshank spots the slight movement, *Corophium volutator* won't have long to live. The tip of the redshank's bill – like the bill tips of most waders – is flexible and sensitive. It can feel for tiny invertebrates, sense movement, and grasp and tug.

We found worms in our sieves. The lugworm digs the deepest and widest hole, a U-shaped burrow which it strengthens with body mucus. It swallows mud, digests the edible stuff, and leaves casts of the waste matter in the shape of coils at the top of one opening of its tunnel. A lugworm is plump-bodied and bristly; its thirteen pairs of red feathery gills extract oxygen. Probably it can only be reached by the long bill of the curlew in hard weather when it retreats deepest – the bill of the female is longer than that of the male.

But all mud-living creatures have to emerge for oxygen and food at intervals. Bacteria use up the oxygen in the mud; the sea brings in fresh supplies only twice a day. Worms retreat into their holes as the mud dries out. Waders must snap them up before they have time to burrow down far.

More worms: a blood-red round worm, a colourful ragworm with bristled segments and a red 'line' (a blood vessel beneath the thin skin) running down the length of its back, and a catworm – not a tube-dweller, but an active free-moving predatory carnivore with a reversible proboscis and sharp teeth.

One mollusc: a Baltic tellin, a burrowing creature with an oval shell.

We looked at our mud-besmeared selves. How did waders keep their plumage in such immaculate condition? How did they manage to step so daintily, never getting stuck, whilst prodding and probing for those shrimps and worms and tellins? No wonder they spend so much time preening.

As we splodged to the nearest rain puddle to clean our wellies, and to do a little preening ourselves before climbing back into the mini-bus, we were full of admiration for the skills of mudflat birds.

Secret Water

Hamford Water, Essex

'Got my "dunderlings" sorted out at last,' said my companion in a satisfied voice.

On the beach below us wintering sanderlings and dunlins, both small short-legged wader species, foraged in a mixed flock. We were on The Naze, Essex's only headland. Behind lay the marshes and Hamford Water.

'The sanderlings have dark edges to their folded wings,' she told me, 'and look at that speckling on the throat of the dunlins.'

I looked. She was right. Whilst I had been relying on 'jizz', comparing the different methods of feeding of the two little birds (sanderling, like little wound-up clockwork toys, fast-speed across the sand, legs a blur, bill-darting at wave edges; dunlin, heads down, shoulders hunched, beak-jab at the sand leaving a little trail of dots, short runs, short walks) she had been studying plumage – confusingly alike in winter, once the dunlin has lost its black belly patch.

This was Arthur Ransome's *Secret Water* country. I was an avid reader of all his books as a child, and he managed to convey, with unobtrusive skill, his own enthusiasm for birdwatching. I remember reading with mounting interest his description of the dipper watched by a thrilled Titty on a lonely hillside in the Lakes . . . and the account of children versus wicked egg collectors after the eggs of the rare diver, on a remote Scottish island in *Great Northern*. Tim Gudgeon, with his Bird Protection Society in *Coot Club* was probably responsible for many of us joining the Royal Society for the Protection of Birds in later years!

Today I was reliving past bookworm hours spent in the company of the Swallows and Amazons as they mapped the Secret Archipelago behind Walton on the Naze, and put names to the islands, dykes, gullies, marshes, spits, fields and creeks.

Arthur Ransome did not get to know the coast of Essex until he was in his fifties. Many of the books which he'd set in the Lakes and on the Norfolk Broads had already been published. He and his wife were still living in the Lake District when they suddenly decided that they would like more exciting sailing and a bigger boat. His success as an author enabled him to buy a 7-ton cutter, the *Nancy Blackett*. They sold (surely with regret) their little boat

Swallow and moved to the Shotley Peninsula which lies between the rivers Orwell and Stour in south Suffolk.

The house they bought was not far, in sailing distance, from Hamford Water. Soon Arthur Ransome was exploring this new territory in the company of friends and their children. He wrote in his autobiography, 'The children camped on Hornsey Island. Tents sprang up. There were fires at night and, during the days, great explorations of all the intricate waters that lie, hidden from the sea, behind the Naze.' A new book was being born, *Secret Water*, published in 1939 – in time to provide escapism for many little evacuees during the War that followed.

As we walked along the top of a dyke wall that day in *Secret Water* country, the water lapped below us, for it was high tide.

'Away to the right of them,' wrote Arthur Ransome, 'they could see the long dyke, curving round the island. Behind them, to the left of them, and in front of them were saltings, reedy marshland, cut up into islands by narrow channels now, soon after high tide, full of water.

' "What's the good of a sea if it's all going to be mud in a few hours," asked Nancy.

' "It's like breathing," said Titty. "Up and down. Up and down. It makes everything alive." '

The Swallows and Amazons followed mastodon hoofprints across the flats, fished for eels, got stranded, and learnt how to walk across the mud on splatchers. We didn't do any of these things – but we *did* see plenty of birds.

Dark-bellied brent geese had gathered at high tide roosts. Small, stocky sooty-black birds, with a white half-collar and a prominent white stern, they would suddenly rise and swirl low over the marshes, their clamouring calls carrying across the water.

'It sounds like, "I'm going, I'm going, I'm going,",' decided someone.

On their long flight from the coastal plains of arctic Siberia, this noisy communicating must serve to keep flocks together. Thousands settle in Britain for the winter, on the Wash and on east and south coast estuaries as far round as the Exe. Brents are the most maritime of the geese, never far from the sea. They feed on the strap-like leaves of eel grass, on other plants of the saltmarsh and, later in the winter, on fields of cereal. In Britain, we are responsible, between November and March each year, for almost half of the world population of the dark-bellied race of brents.

We watched the geese as they moved restlessly, settling and resettling. Once landed, they stretched, shook their wings vigorously, made little mock-aggressive rushes at each other, preened, fed and rested. But at all times they remained vigilant, easily disturbed – very wary.

Shelduck were feeding in the creek. A little grebe swam across, riding the choppy water, past a moored sailing boat and three yellow buoys. A redshank, squidging over the thin line of fringe mud still uncovered, uncharacteristically allowed us to approach so close that we were able to see its white eyerings.

The tide turned. Strings of waders flew back to feed as the water retreated from the dykes and saltmarsh: oystercatcher, lapwing, ringed plover, grey plover, turnstone, bar-tailed godwit, snipe, sanderling and dunlin. (Arthur Ransome called dunlins 'ox-birds', a local Essex name for them.) Two herons landed and stood surveying the scene, taking stock. A shag flew swiftly down the length of a channel and disappeared round a bend.

Then a short-eared owl rose up. Quartering the flat ground of the saltmarsh on long rounded wings, it flew low, backwards and forwards, vole-detecting. Of a sudden it braked, twisted, pounced – then lifted up again, to resume its to-and-fro search: the owl most likely to be seen hunting during daylight hours.

Flocks of greenfinches twittered their way in front of us, taking advantage of small shrubs to perch on, bathing in shallow pools below. Skylarks, a pied wagtail, reed buntings – and rock pipits on the landward side of the sea wall. And on the estuary side – small flocks of twite.

We had hoped very much to see twite and, as it turned out, our wish had been granted very quickly. The first sighting was in the car park on arrival. 'What's that small brown job?' someone asked as we got out of the coach. It was a twite, enjoying an energetic splashing in a rain puddle.

'Small brown job' is an unfair description. The breast of a twite is a streaky yellow ochre, and there is pink on the back above the tail in the male. The light was good and the stubby yellow bill caught the sun. Twite winter in huge numbers on Essex saltings after breeding in summer on heathery uplands. In small parties they congregate, seed-searching on the saltmarsh below the dyke walls

'Next time, a mastodon?'

Beyond the reedbeds of the landward side flocks of black-headed gulls, lapwing and wood pigeons fed in ploughed fields. On stubble, grey partridge (orange head and black horseshoe on breast) and red-legged partridge (larger, with a white face and black neck-bib) pecked at left-over grain. Disturbed by a passer-by, they whirred low over the furrows. From the hedgerow flew a dozen redwing with chestnut flanks and creamy eyestripes.

We reached the sandy shore of The Naze. We saw – and sorted out – the 'dunderlings'. Dunlin we had observed earlier in muddy creeks, but sanderling are strictly birds of the sandy shore.

Glistening wet, wrack-covered, wave-lapped rocks served as look-out posts for gulls – great black-backed and black-headed. One mystery gull had us puzzled. Until we decided that it must be a solitary kittiwake at a curious stage in feather moult.

Not much of a mystery. But in Arthur Ransome country a mystery is obligatory and it was the best we could do. Next time, perhaps, a boat, splatchers and a hunt for a mastodon?

Swan Lake

Slimbridge New Grounds, Gloucestershire

Through the huge picture windows of the entrance foyer we could see that the pools were almost frozen over. Ducks waddled awkwardly on webbed feet like nervous little old ladies afraid of skidding on the ice.

We hurried through the grounds and reached the tall Acrow Tower. We climbed the wooden steps to the top. Icy winds howled and swept piercingly through the gaps in the slats. But at 51 feet above the ground we were able to enjoy a magnificent view of the Severn Estuary and Bristol Channel.

During the summer months cattle and sheep graze on the banks, their numbers carefully regulated. As winter approaches, the stock is moved further inland. The whole area is given over completely to thousands of in-flying wildfowl and waders which have come to know it as a safe refuge. Security patrols ensure non-disturbance; fields are fertilised, or even resown if the quality or correct species composition of grasses diminishes; the Severn/Trent River Authority has excavated four shallow scrapes which are planted with food and, in some years, enriched with slurry; wheat supplements are distributed twice daily in the Rushy Pen and Swan Lake areas.

A little owl sat on a fence, its feathers fluffed out against the cold. A merlin swooped and settled, becoming just a dot in the middle of the field. Skeins of geese flew over. Two thousand wigeon swirled, whistling, to land on the ice of the frozen canal in a great jostling crowd. Gradually they spread themselves over the banks and into the pastures to graze on either side.

'There were the Bewick's.'

And *there* were the Bewick's at the edge of the estuary, small swans – not much more than half the size of our native mute swans – and brilliantly white.

Bewick's swans winter each year in long-established, traditional European sites. The Ouse Washes is one such site; up to 4,500 gather on the Wildfowl Trust's Welney Refuge. Bewick's were persuaded to accept Slimbridge as a new winter haunt shortly after its beginnings on the reclaimed land of the eastern bank of the Severn Estuary in 1946. The presence of whistling swans (close relations) in the Slimbridge collection and, later, a few tame Bewick's, enticed down on to the Dumbles a scattering of individuals from an over-flying flock – probably on its way to Ireland. Numbers increased annually until, nowadays, wintering Bewick's swans can be counted in hundreds.

Swan 'personalities' have made the headlines. On the day of our visit the STOP-SPOT board in the foyer read: 'Lady Harold returns'. So she was back again, all the way back from her Siberian breeding grounds 2,300 miles away – in spite of everything.

As an inexpert young swan – several years previously – she had crashed through the dining room window of the Director's house on the edge of Swan Lake, shattering glass and badly lacerating a wing. An eminent surgeon, by chance in the members' observatory at the time, saw the accident happen. If it hadn't been for Sir Harold's fortunate presence, it is doubtful if the yearling would have survived. But the story is by now well known – how she flew back with her herd to Russia – to forgive and to return again, year after year, to Slimbridge.

Bewick's swans can be recognised by the individual black and yellow patterning on their bills. Like the fingerprints of a human, the marks are infinitely variable. At Slimbridge dossiers are kept, with drawings of bill patterns, of as many swans as possible. Each is given a name (so much easier to memorise than a number).

There have been other personalities. 'Lancelot is back,' read the notice in the foyer winter after winter. Lancelot is, perhaps, even more famous than Lady Harold. He was among the first to take advantage of the new landscaped pool close to the observatory and soon to be christened Swan Lake. Each year, he returned. His first two wives, Victoria and Grail, died in accidents. He found a third wife, Elaine. For twenty-three consecutive years he flew back and forth from the USSR with his wives and, occasionally, with cygnets too (although Lancelot was assessed 'a poor breeder'). It wasn't until the winter of 1986/7 that the sad news was reported in *Wildfowl World*, 'Lancelot goes missing'. Elaine had arrived on her own. First recorded as an adult bird, he must have reached at least twenty-five years and so had probably died of old age. The following year, 1987/8, Elaine flew in – with a new mate.

And there are other remarkable swans which keep returning; 'Prongy', 'Greytel', 'Ku', 'Cuba', 'Offset', 'Quixote', 'Blackbird' and his pen, 'Thrush' . . . all have their own dossiers.

But back to that winter-past snowy day when we watched the Bewick's swans from Acrow Hide until our noses were blue with cold and our fingers, frozen in their mitts. Then I remembered that, as an associate member of the Trust, I am entitled to use the 'members' observatory'. It was good to find the observatory snug and warm, centrally heated and welcoming. The view from the huge windows on to Swan Lake was spectacular.

Through large sheets of glass we looked out on to the lake, a 'jumbo birdtable' which, each night, attracts wild birds at dusk up from the shores of the Severn. Snow on the banks, floating ice, orange-red pollarded willows on small islands, distant views of snow-covered fields – and graceful white swans.

As the light began to fade, there was a great rushing of wings and a tremendous hullabaloo of trumpetings, honkings, squawkings and quackings as more wildfowl – flocks of ducks and geese, herds of Bewick's – headed for Swan Lake.

They settled in front of us (underwater heating keeps the water free of sheet ice) and waited in anticipation for the warden to trundle out with his loaded wheelbarrow and to scatter wheat and barley, the nightly ritual. The babble of noise rose to a deafening crescendo. Dozens of teal upended, displaying yellow sterns. Pintail, shoveler, pochard, wigeon – zoomed in, scudding low over the water, landing inelegantly.

Barnacle geese charged with outstretched necks. Mallards waddled along the shore gobbling up overlooked grains. Along the edges crept hopeful coot. Bewick swans were still flying up from the estuary. They splashed down, wonderful wild birds from the wide open spaces of the north; they dipped long necks, and picked the food from the floor of the lake as it fell into the water and sank.

And slowly, enhancing the scene, the orange ball of the sun dropped below the horizon leaving the sky ablaze with pink, and turning the snow to pink, and the white plumage of the beautiful swans.

Winter Atlas
South Leicestershire

For three winters in succession I went counting birds on 'frosty winds made moan, earth stood hard as iron' days for the British Trust for Ornithology's *Winter Atlas* project. The purpose of the scheme was to record the precise distribution of all bird species wintering in Britain and Ireland. Millions fly here to escape adverse conditions in Europe, Asia and the Arctic. There are movements within Britain from high ground to low, and to estuaries from inland rivers and lakes. 'Cold weather movements' occur if the weather worsens; more continental birds fly in; British birds move south or west.

The British Trust for Ornithology asked volunteers to survey 10-kilometre squares of the National Grid from mid-November to the end of February for three consecutive winters, 1981/2, 1982/3, 1983/4.

The BTO, staffed by professionals, has a tradition of relying heavily on 'informed amateurs'.

'Many observers find a seemingly insatiable fascination in atlas fieldwork, which appears to fulfil all that is best in competitiveness and "collecting" whilst at the same time providing a fitting tool for co-operative study and the amassing of distributional data,' writes I.J. Ferguson-Lees in '*Enjoying Ornithology: a celebration of the British Trust for Ornithology 1933 – 1983*'. (edited by R.A.O. Hickling.)

Which perhaps explains why I was prepared to abandon my cosy central heating, don my duffle coat, thickest corduroys and wellington boots and, with a companion, brave the icy blasts of Leicestershire's open countryside to count wintering birds.

The winter of 1981/2 was exceptionally hard. Conditions were severe with Leicestershire canals frozen, tow paths knee-deep in snow, vegetation iced over. The following two winters were classified average/mild.

We marched briskly along winding country lanes, trudged across snowswept fields, stood shivering in woodland, prowled along hedgerows, slithered on the mud of bridle paths and peered over walls into cottage gardens and farmyard middens.

The pair of us sorted out as best we could distant flocks of rooks? crows? and those far-off difficult gulls: black-headed? common? herring? lesser black-backed? We puzzled together over the inevitable 'mystery' birds.

The count was my responsibility, but it was good to have Reenie alongside to assure me that my 'guesstimates' of huge gatherings of lapwings, starlings and wood pigeons were not too wildly way out whilst I filled up the record cards, noting the total number seen of each species and the date, weather conditions – and time spent out in the field.

We couldn't, of course, begin to draw any conclusions from our random sightings. That was the job of the computer at Tring. But I will write of a typical morning in December, and the birds we noted in the bleak Leicestershire landscape that day.

We drove out through Wigston along the A50, and stopped near Kilby Bridge. Fields on either side of the road held large flocks of lapwing, fieldfare, black-headed gulls, starlings and wood pigeons – and we scanned with binoculars for golden plover. Golden plover individuals tend to stand discreetly distanced from each other, each with a need for its own 'personal space'. Yes, a flock of seventeen of the comely spangled birds were in the middle of the far field.

We drove on and turned right for Foston. Beside the little church we found redwing – a Christmas card picture – in the hawthorn hedge; and great tits, blue tits, chaffinches, robins and a wren in the shrubbery.

On to Gumley Wood for woodland birds: goldcrests – tiny fidgets – seeking insects high in the needles of a conifer; a treecreeper spiralling up a long trunk; a small party of five long-tailed tits; and a great spotted woodpecker bounding across an open space over the heads of Jacob sheep.

To Saddington Reservoir for tufted duck, pochard, great crested grebe, coot, heron, Canada geese. Back through Wistow to check for more waterbirds on Wistow Pond. Is the mistle thrush still aggressively guarding 'his' holly tree in Newton Harcourt churchyard? We walk a little way along the towpath of the Grand Union Canal and see a bullfinch with pink breast and bold white tail patch.

Time to return, counting all the way and pausing at the farm with the haystacks which guarantee yellowhammers; and on each canal bridge to check for moorhen, mallard, mute swan; and at the old barn where jackdaws cavort.

Jacob sheep

There have been many memorable moments over the three years. Highlights include a brambling in a flock of assorted finches; thirty-six siskin acrobating in alder trees; five snipe sortieing out from a marsh beside the canal path; and goldfinches in a clump of thistles.

A diminutive lesser spotted woodpecker (black and white stripes, red cap) clung to a tree trunk with spread claws and braced tail only 5 feet above us in a copse near Wistow. And we counted seven mistle thrushes in the company of twenty redwing – the largest and the smallest of our thrushes in one flock.

Birdwatching skills improved with all this practice. It grew easier not to mistake common partridges for clods of earth in a muddy field. Stock doves which, with few distinguishing marks, may easily escape notice, can look very blue and conspicuous on a sunny day especially in a snowy field. I learned to look *down* instead of up for small birds; many species, particularly the tits, bramblings and chaffinches, ground-feed in winter weather, descending from the trees to search for fallen seeds in leaf litter.

We got to know which birds prefer to feed in the shelter of a hedge: blackbird, song thrush, wren, moorhen, dunnock. If there were berries on the hedge, we listened for the loud 'chack' of the fieldfare and the soft 'choop' of redwing.

Even in the worst of weather, blizzards can blow the snow into drifts exposing seedheads of thistle, chickweed, plantain, dock and mugwort. Small birds disappear into igloo-like holes in deep vegetation. Others roost communally, sharing body warmth, sometimes flying into cities where the temperature is higher. A favourite roost for eighty pied wagtails is a Christmas tree put up each year outside a large store in Leicester's city centre; they flit in and out, lit by the tree's fairy lights, and very pretty decorations they make.

Winter Atlas perks were rewarding. If it hadn't been for my commitment I might never have discovered the tiny tenth-century church, with its rounded Norman arches . . . or the Anglo-Saxon 'hollow way' . . . or the stretch of straight track built by the Romans. An eighteenth-century canal settlement with wharves for the unloading of coal with its own Navigation Inn, a deserted 'enclosure act' village and the oldest man-made sheet of water in the county: we discovered them all in square SP69.

We watched hares racing across a frosty field – and grey squirrels nut-hunting in a fox covert – and huntsmen in bright red jackets galloping across fields below.

We enjoyed intricate leaf patterns contrived by hoar frost, whiskery grey cascades of old man's beard tumbling over a twiggy hedge and the spooky silence of swirling fog. We saw how emerald green moss and orange lichen emphasise the lettering on old gravestones. We found cobwebs beautifully bespangled with dew, and robin's pincushions, witches' brooms and other strange galls.

Each day I put out food for the birds in my SP69 garden. So many small birds came to feed that a kestrel was attracted. Driven by hunger, it killed and ate a starling – one of a feeding flock of thirty – in the snow just two feet away from my french window. A swoosh . . . a squawk . . . and the kestrel had the bird in its talons and killed it on the spot, ignoring my close presence.

For a few bitter 'glazing days' in the worst of the winters, four brambling, five chaffinches, eight blackbirds, a song thrush, a dozen reed buntings (nineteen ˙on one memorable day) up to fourteen greenfinches and ten collared doves – as well as the regulars, blue tits, great tits, coal tits, robin, house sparrows, dunnocks and starlings – made use of the garden as a feeding station.

Birds fluffed out their feathers for warmth as they waited for me to top up peanut holders and seed dispensers. Black-headed gulls swooped to snatch bones from the Christmas turkey carcass. Squirrels roused themselves to raid the bird table – and then vanished again for days to sleep off the effects of the meal. A fieldfare 'took over' the garden in one cold snap, hogging the damaged apples I had put out and driving away resident blackbirds. A single siskin turned up at a winter's end, in March, to swing on the red peanut bag.

Wood pigeons arrived to gobble up scattered wild bird seed. A pied wagtail appreciated put-out water.

We finished our *Winter Atlas* Count in style on 29 February, 1984: five tree sparrows on a manure heap; a jay and a treecreeper in full view both at the same time; the largest count yet of fieldfare (620) and almost the largest of lapwing (4,600). A yellowhammer sang from a hawthorn twig songpost, staking his claim to territory, and a skylark, too, was in song.

In fact, so noisy were the birds on that last day it seemed they didn't know about Leap Year. To them it was already March, the start of Spring and an excuse for vocal celebration. Our counting for the *Winter Atlas* had come to an end and we felt quite sad. Each year we had witnessed the first white snowdrops and the first yellow aconites; the first golden catkins of hazel and silver catkins of pussy willow; the first new-born lamb; and the first chocolate brown cap of a black-headed gull.

But we can relive it all over again as, today, we turn the pages of the published *BTO Atlas of Wintering Birds*. We look at the dots on the county of Leicestershire and 'see' again the gorgeous colours of fieldfare and redwing feeding on red berries in a snowy surround – and those golden blobs of yellowhammers in a hoar-frosted hedgerow.

Early aconites

Acknowledgements

Thank you to all my good friends in the RSPB Leicester Group, the Leicestershire and Rutland Ornithological Society, the Leicestershire and Rutland Trust for Nature Conservation, the Natural History Section of the Leicester Literary and Philosophical Society and the Leicester Writers' Club.

In particular I should like to thank Simon Carter, Jan Dawson, Peter Dean, Ken Goodrich, Dennis Hemsley, Jean Ironside and Bert Smith – and all the other members of the hard-working outings committees – for giving so generously of their time to organise enjoyable outings year round and in all compass directions.

A special thank you to Dr Marjorie Gibbons ('MBG') for introducing me to birdwatching; to Rod Baker, Bob Cherry, Dave Cohen, Rod Cox, Dave Gamble, Alan Jones, Peter Kightley, Fred Littlemore, Chris Measures, Barry Raine, Dave Smallshire and Doreen Thompson for their first-rate leadership on outings; and to all those who so good-naturedly share their knowledge and observations: Keith Allsopp, John Bielby, Reenie Clay, Trevor Davies, Angela and Peter Davis, Pat and Ian Evans, Stuart Gill, David Harper, Tom Hering, Ron Hickling, Mark Holling, Jack Otter, Pauline Rose, Dave Scott, Geoff Stansfield, John Thatcher . . . and many more, including those mentioned elsewhere in the text.

Reenie Clay and Dave Cohen kindly read, and commented upon, an early draft of the script; I am indebted to Martin Withers for his beautiful colour photographs of the kingfisher, gannets and great spotted woodpecker, and I am also extremely grateful for the help I have received from the Field Studies Council, Gibraltar Point Field Station, Nature Conservancy Council, Royal Society for Nature Conservation, Royal Society for the Protection of Birds and the Wildfowl Trust.

Magazine Acknowledgements

Some of the material in *Birdwatcher's Year* first appeared in the following magazines: *Camping and Caravanning*, *The Dalesman*, *The Field*, *Good Housekeeping*, *Home and Country*, *The Lady*, *Lincolnshire Life*, *New Scientist*, *RSPCA Today*, *SHE*, *Waterways World* and *Western Mail*.

Useful Addresses

British Trust for Conservation Volunteers (BTCV), 36 St Mary's Street, Wallingford, Oxford OX10 OEU

British Trust for Ornithology, Beech Grove, Tring, Hertforshire HP23 2NR

Camping and Caravanning Club, 11 Grosvenor Place, London SW1W 0EY

Central Electricity Generating Board, The Surveyor, Sudbury House, 15 Newgate Street, London EC1A 7AU

Field Studies Council, Information Officer, Preston Montford, Montford Bridge, Shrewsbury, Shropshire SY4 1HW

Forestry Commission, 231 Corstorphine Road, Edinburgh EH12 7AT

Gibraltar Point Field Station, near Skegness, Lincolnshire

Gloucestershire Trust for Nature Conservation, Church House, Standish, Stonehouse, Glos. GL10 3EV

John Clare Society, 8 Priory Road, Peterborough, Cambridgeshire

Leicestershire and Rutland Ornithological Society, Chris Measures, 28 Oakfield Road, Birstall, Leicestershire LE4 3DQ

Leicestershire and Rutland Trust for Nature Conservation, 1 West Street, Leicester LE1 6UU

Lincolnshire and South Humberside Trust for Nature Conservation, The Manor House, Alford, Lincolnshire LN13 9DL

Nature Conservancy Council, 19-20 Belgrave Square, London SW1X 8PY

National Trust, 42 Queen Anne's Gate, London SW1H 9AS

Norfolk Naturalists' Trust, 72 Cathedral Close, Norwich, Norfolk NR1 4DF

Ramblers' Association, 1-5 Wandsworth Road, London SW8 2XX

Royal Society for Nature Conservation, 22 The Green, Nettleham, Lincoln LN2 2NR

Royal Society for the Protection of Birds, The Lodge, Sandy, Bedfordshire

RSPB Leicester Members' Group, Peter Kightley, 16 Barwell Road, Kirby Muxloe, Leicester LE9 9AA

Suffolk Trust for Nature Conservation, Park Cottage, Saxmundham, Suffolk IP17 1DQ

West Wales Naturalists' Trust (now the Dyfed Wildlife Trust), 7 Market Street, Haverfordwest, Dyfed

Wildfowl Trust, Slimbridge, Gloucester GL2 7BT

Woodland Trust, Westgate, Grantham, Lincolnshire NG31 6LL

Yorkshire Wildlife Trust, 3rd Floor, 10 Toft Green, off Micklegate, York YO1 1JT

Further Reading

Axell, Bert and Hosking, Eric. *Minsmere: Portrait of a Bird Reserve* (Hutchinson, 1977)

Bang, Preben and Dahlstrom, Preben. *Collins Guide to Animal Tracks and Signs* (Collins, 1974)

Barrett, John. *The Pembrokeshire Coastal Path* (HMSO, 1974)

Barrett, John and Yonge, C. M. *The Pocket Guide to the Seashore* (Collins, 1972)

Bruun, Bertel. *The Hamlyn Guide to Birds of Britain and Europe* (Hamlyn, 1970)

Chapman, Anthony (editor). *RSPB Reserves Visiting* (Christopher Helm, 1987)

Clare, John. *Bird Poems* (The Folio Society, 1980)

Clarke, W. G. *In Breckland Wilds* (Robert Scott, 1925)

Conder, Peter. *RSPB Guide to Birdwatching* (Hamlyn, 1982)

Condry, William. *The Natural History of Wales*, The New Naturalist (Collins, 1981)

Cramp, Stanley *et al* (editors). *Handbook of the Birds of Europe, the Middle East and North Africa: the Birds of the Western Palearctic* (seven volumes) (Oxford University Press)

Davies, Stan. *Wildlife of the Exe Estuary* (Dartmouth: Harbour Books, 1983)

Durman, Roger. *Bird Observatories in Britain and Ireland* (T. & A. D. Poyser, 1976)

Elkins, Norman. *Weather and Bird Behaviour* (Poyser, 1983)

Ferguson-Lee, James *et al*. *The Shell Guide to the Birds of Britain and Ireland* (Michael Joseph, 1983)

Fitter, Richard and Blamey, Marjorie. *The Wild Flowers of Britain and Northern Europe* (Collins, 1974)

Flegg, Jim. *The Puffin* (Shire Natural History, 1985)

Freare, Christopher. *The Starling* (Shire Natural History, 1984)

Fuller, R. J. *Bird Habitats in Britain* (T. & A. D. Poyser, 1982)

Glue, David (editor). *The Garden Bird Book* (BTO/Macmillan, 1982)

Gooders, John. *Where to Watch Birds in Britain and Europe* (Andre Deutsch, 1970)

Gooders, John. *The New Where to Watch Birds* (Andre Deutsch, 1986)

Greenoak, Francesca. *All the Birds of the Air* (Andre Deutsch, 1979)

Hale, W. G. *Waders*, The New Naturalist (Collins, 1980)

Hayman, Peter and Burton, Philip. *The Birdlife of Britain and Europe* (Revised edition, 1986)

Heinzel, H., Fitter, R. and Parslow, J. *The Birds of Britain and Europe* (Collins, 1985)

Hickling, Ronald (editor). *Enjoying Ornithology: A Celebration of Fifty Years of The British Trust for Ornithology* (T. & A. D. Poyser, 1983)

Hickling, Ronald. *Birds in Leicestershire and Rutland* (LROS, 1978)

Hill, Mike and Langsbury, Gordon. *A Field Guide to Photographing Birds in Britain and Western Europe* (Collins, 1987)

Hywel-Davies, Jeremy and Thom, Valerie. *The Macmillan Guide to Britain's Nature Reserves* (Macmillan Papermac, 1986)

Jackman, Brian. *The Countryside in Winter* (Hutchinson, 1985)

Kingsley, Charles. *The Water Babies* (Blackie and Son Ltd, 1863)

Lack, Peter. *The Atlas of Wintering Birds in Britain and Ireland* (T. & A. D. Poyser/ BTO, 1986)

Lloyd, E. R. *The Wild Red Deer of Exmoor* (The Exmoor Press, 1970)

Lloyd, Francis Ernest. *The Carnivorous Plants* (Dover, 1976)

Lockley, Ronald. *The Island* (Andre Deutsch, 1969)

McLellan, Robert. *The Isle of Arran* (David & Charles, 1970)

Meade, Chris. *Bird Migration* (Country Life, 1983)

Nelson, Bryan. *The Gannet* (T. & A. D. Poyser, 1978)

Nethersole-Thompson, Desmond and Mamie. *Waders: their Breeding, Haunts and Watchers* (T. & A. D. Poyser, 1986)

Newton, Ian. *Finches*, The New Naturalist (Collins, 1972)·

Nicholson, E. M. *The Art of Birdwatching* (Witherby, 1931)

Oddie, William. *Bill Oddie's Little Black Bird Book* (Methuen, 1980)

Ogilvie, Malcolm. *The New Guide to Wetlands in Britain* (David & Charles, 1979)

Peterson, Roger T., Mountfort, Guy and Hollom, P. A. D. *A Field Guide to the Birds of Britain and Europe* (Collins, 1983)

Phillips, Roger, *Common and Important Mushrooms* (Elm Tree Books, 1986)

Prater, A. J. *Estuary Birds of Britain and Ireland* (T. & A. D. Poyser, 1981)

Ransome, Arthur. *Coot Club* (Jonathan Cape, 1934)

Ransome, Arthur. *Great Northern* (Jonathan Cape, 1947)

Ransome, Arthur. *Secret Water* (Jonathan Cape, 1939)

Rayner, R. W. (editor). *The Natural History of Pagham Harbour – Part 1 & 2* (Bognor Regis Natural Science Society Publications, 1979 & 1981)

Richards, Alan. *British Birds: a Field Guide* (David & Charles, 1982)

Richards, Alan. *The Birdwatcher's A-Z* (David & Charles, 1981)

Robinson, Eric and Fitter, Richard (editors). *John Clare's Birds* (OUP, 1982)

Sharrock, J. T. R. (compiler). *The Atlas of Breeding Birds in Britain and Ireland* (BTO/ T. & A. D. Poyser, 1976)

Simms, Eric. *British Thrushes*, The New Naturalist (Collins, 1978)

Scott, Peter. *Observations of Wildlife* (Phaidon, 1980)

Sills, Norman (compiler). *Titchwell Marsh: the First Ten Years* (RSPB, 1983)

Soper, Tony. *The Bird Table Book in Colour* (David & Charles, 1978)

South, Richard. *The Moths of the British Isles* (Warne, 1961)

Storey, Edward. *A Right to Song: the Life of John Clare* (Methuen, 1982)

Thomas, J. A. *RSNC Guide to Butterflies of the British Isles* (1986)

Watson, Donald. *The Hen Harrier* (T. & A. D. Poyser, 1977)

Periodicals

Birds – magazine of the Royal Society for the Protection of Birds

Bird Study – the journal of the British Trust for Ornithology

Bird Watching – monthly magazine

British Birds – monthly journal from Fountains, Park Lane, Blunham, Bedford MK44 2NJ

BTO News – newsletter of the British Trust for Ornithology

John Clare Society Journal – published annually

Natural World – magazine of the Royal Society for Nature Conservation

Wildfowl World – a magazine for members of The Wildfowl Trust

Index